The Python Programming Revolution

Scripting Success: Practical Approaches to Python Programming

David Lee

Table of Contents

INTRODUCTION

Python is one of the most potent, adjustable programming languages that are very highly used in various industries today. From its usage in web development to automation, with data science and artificial intelligence covering it all, it is dominated significantly by Python as the choice of language for developers across all levels. This is all because it is easy to use and effective. This is an all-inclusive bookwork, "The Python Programming Revolution: Scripting Success: Practical Approaches to Python Programming," for learning the nitty-gritty in programming with very practical approaches that are strongly rooted in reality.

Whether you are just starting to learn how to program or looking to refresh your memory with Python, this book will nicely guide you through the basic ideas. Starting from the very basics of the syntax of Python to object-oriented programming, data structures, and file handling, all is done in great detail. Each chapter is designed not only to describe features of Python but also to demonstrate how to apply them within a variety of coding contexts.

Our final objective is to give you the knowledge and arsenal of tools that will enable you to exploit all the power offered by Python, so that you might successfully get through programming as well as become a real expert script writer. By the end of reading this book, you will make clean, efficient Python code that you can apply to your work: automation of any kind personal to business processes, solving real-world problems, or contributing to innovative projects in various industries.

CHAPTER I

Basic Python Programming

The Evolution and Importance of Python

One of the most widely used programming languages by most people around the world was born a long time ago, in all its greatness and not known for making a large sensation. Therefore, it may surprise one to discover that one of the languages seeing an increasingly steep growth curve since its inception is that which was developed by Guido van Rossum in the late 1980s: Python. Due to its simplicity, readability, and versatility, it remains an essential tool for programmers at every skill level working in fields such as web development, data science, artificial intelligence, and much more. It is only when one explores the history of Python, its design philosophies, how it has evolved in time, and the reasons why it seems so apt in today's fast-paced technological environment that one appreciates exactly how highly significant this language is.

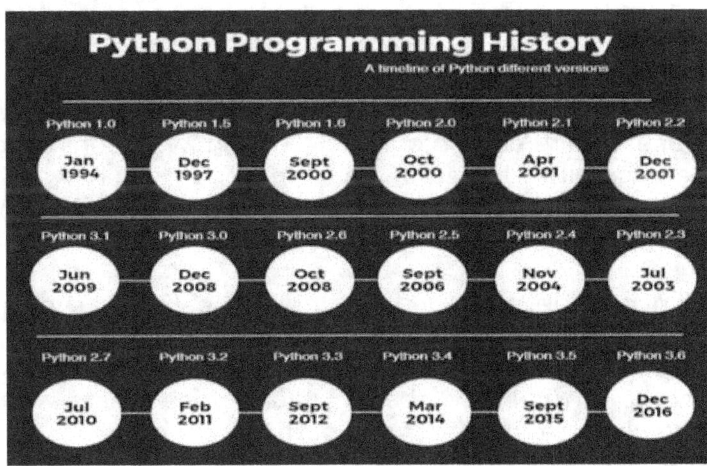

Guido van Rossum, a Dutch programmer, came up with the idea of creating Python at the end of the 1980s. It was originally conceived as an alternative for the ABC programming language that was first thought of to be used more for teaching and prototyping purposes but had drawbacks that prevented general adoption. Working at the Centrum Wiskunde & Informatica (CWI), a research institute in the Netherlands, Van Rossum had aimed at developing a language of such nature to correct the weaknesses of ABC while retaining the good features like readability and simplicity. He was interested in developing a language for system management as well as scripting which could be used for accomplishing even more complex jobs but remain easy to learn. The first version was named after the British comic troupe Monty Python and released in 1991 because Van Rossum wanted Python to be fun to work with.

Python was designed from scratch with a distinct, well-defined aim: to make code readable and usable. The "Zen of Python," which espouses this spirit, enumerates maxims such as "beautiful is better than ugly," "explicit is better than implicit," and "simple is better than complex." These maxims have ensured that Python has remained a language appropriate for beginners yet still has depth and functionality that serious developers demand. It is readable, code blocks are identified by use of indentation rather than brackets or other punctuation marks, and it was especially appealing to people who wanted to produce clean, readable code. Python was considered more accessible because of its method, which was far removed from the syntactical complexity of many languages in use at the time.

Python was developed throughout the 1990s. The first major milestone for Python came in 1994: Python 1.0. At this point, the essential elements-functions, exception handling, and those basic data types that would eventually form the backbone of the language-were included. Python benefited from a dynamic and expanding community of developers because Python is open-source software. Its open-source nature was key to its rapid development and widespread adoption. This community-driven approach would eventually be institutionally codified through the Python Software Foundation, established in 2001, which ensured that the development of the language would continue to be open and community-based. Added in Python 2.0, released in early 2000, were such important features as garbage collection, list comprehensions, and improved Unicode support. However, Python 2.x became a ubiquitous tool for scientific computing as well as web programming. Still, its designers thought that some features were too weak. In Python 3.0, designed to achieve this goal, was released in 2008. Python 3 Cleaning up inconsistencies and throwing out features out of date were aimed for the release of Python 3. Although not backward-compatible with Python 2, some developers initially shunned Python 3, even with the advancements it offered, and hence unwilling to update their applications. However, time told, and the community grew to favor Python 3 due to its better memory management, clearer syntax, and improved Unicode handling. It is therefore that in 2020, Python 2 was declared officially abandoned.

One major turning point that has molded the history of this language is its transition to Python 3, sealing its place in the list of the most advanced and efficient programming languages of today. Due to the great flexibility, it offers, the pace at which technology develops, followed by Python as well in subsequent years after Python 3 was released, increased tremendously its usage cases. Python has become popular and important because of the vast size of its standard library and an immense third-party library and framework community. Dealing with files, regular expressions, and networking have become easier with Python's standard library modules and functions. Yet again, it is through third-party libraries like NumPy, Pandas, and TensorFlow that Python remains one of the first favorites of language when it comes to data analysis, machine learning, and artificial intelligence. No hyperbole is more apt to describe the importance of Python in data science. As the need to take decisions supported by some evidence increased in several sectors, the language became first choice for machine learning and data analysis. Because it was straightforward, data scientists could concentrate on algorithms and data rather than getting bogged down in complex syntax, and libraries such as NumPy and Pandas presented several ways to quickly manipulate and analyze large datasets, besides which informative data visualizations were easily made accessible with the visualization packages in Python, especially Matplotlib and Seaborn. Its position in this industry has been further cemented by the advent of machine learning and AI; it has become relatively easy for developers to design complicated AI models using frameworks like TensorFlow and PyTorch.

The capabilities of Python go beyond mere data science. It has grown to be one of the cornerstones in the realm of online programming, with frameworks such as Flask and Django having it so easy to create scalable, fault-tolerant web applications. More to the point, though, is that Django provides a high-level framework that promotes efficient development and clear, practical design. Much like software projects of every size benefit from Python's readability and simplicity, the language's ability to integrate well with other technologies and databases makes it a critically important tool in any kind of backend development environment. Another place where Python really shines is in automation. Very large library support and easy syntax make Python a very effective language in which to automate tasks. From renaming files and downloading data to creating highly complex systems for automating corporation activities, Python is gradually becoming an unprecedented automation variable. Python's simplicity and flexibility for use in administering systems and network programming make configuration management, server provisioning, and other critical activities take a backseat and require minimal effort on the part of the administrator.

Python also manifests in teaching and novice programming. This is one of the best programming languages that can be used to teach programming fundamentals because it's highly readable and has a very low entrance fee to get started with it. It has become a prominent tool both in educational institutes and online coding environments such as Codecademy and edX, where novice programmers are exposed to the world of coding. Due to its syntax being very close to plain English, beginners may easily acquire the logic of programming without being intimidated by the complexities of languages such as Java or C++. Popularity in education has encouraged a new generation of coders who start their programming career with a language that not only teaches them the basics but grows with their requirements when they advance to more sophisticated projects. Such factors as an open-source platform and a strong supporting community have been the core towards the sustained momentum of Python. The Python community is well-known for an open-friendliness, cooperation, and knowledge exchange environment. This gives a large number of resources, guides, documentation, tutorials, and forums for developers from any level of experience. Another much more important feature of the Python world is the possibility for developers to exchange and to use others' code within the Python Package Index (PyPI)-it contains hundreds of third-party packages. Each year, developers of Python meet at the PyCon conference, held all across the globe.

It is a place to share ideas with one another, present work done, and discuss plans for the language in question.

Apart from technical advantages, cross-platform portability and wide-scale adoption among major software organizations have greatly affected the technology world. Among these companies, the using ones include Google, Instagram, Spotify, Netflix, and many others. They use it in machine learning, data processing, and backend infrastructure. Google has been rather more aggressive in marketing Python and thus, it is one of the three officially supported languages besides C++ and Java. Besides all this flexibility, another plus point is that it can also interface with other languages, such as C, C++, and JavaScript. This gives a lot of additional power to it as developers can use the benefits of Python at specific moments and use other tools elsewhere. Python represents the dawn of big data, machine learning, and artificial intelligence. The tool has become crucial for developers, data scientists, and engineers due to the surge in automation and increasing importance of data-driven decision-making. As such, Python is to point the way of innovation in technology for decades to come with strong features and unprecedented usability. The "fame" of the code as well as the constantly enlarging ecosystem in Python and the constant development suit it to keep up with new breakthroughs in areas such as cybersecurity, bioinformatics, or quantum computing.

In summary, evidence of the flexibility of Python, the design ethos, and community-driven development is its rise from the original straightforward scripting language to the new pinnacle in modern programming. While its is due to the power and versatility that Python has landed itself into everything-from-web development to data analysis, automation to artificial intelligence- domains it is simplicity and readability that made it the most preferred choice among the freshers. However, the software world grows at such an incredible pace; the fact that Python can adapt to new technologies, and in support of an endless list of libraries and frameworks makes this language so relevant in the fast-evolving tech scene. It is undoubtedly one of the most important programming languages of our day and will only become more so as long as the industries continuously use it in cutting-edge applications.

Setting Up Your Python Environment

The configuration of your environment is one of the first steps toward learning the language and trust in Python programming. A good environment improves flow and productivity while developing. Being very flexible and applicable, Python can be set up on all operating systems: Windows, macOS, or Linux. Installing Python is done in each system, to some tooling and best practices, so the development experience goes with fewer rejection. The section passes through the proper installation of a Python environment in the installation of Python, setting up an Integrated Development Environment (IDE), administration of packages as well as their dependencies, and how to understand virtual environments. These steps drive the heart of a stable and effective Python development setup.

The first thing to do in setting up Python is to install the language itself. And there are two huge versions of Python that can be installed: Python 2 and Python 3. Since Python 2 is no longer in life as of this year 2020, Python 3 is recommended for new projects. Therefore, I should have Python 3 installed since it supports modern features, has better syntax, and is way more efficient. It's free to get Python, and you can download it free from the main www.python.org website for the major operating systems. Installing on Windows will download an installer that will simplify this for you by also installing other additional needed components besides Python. Another not-so-obvious requirement, but just as important, is to add Python on the system path at installation, which then makes it possible to access and use through the command line or terminal.

In general, Python used to come preinstalled in most macOS and Linux systems, but that may be an old version, hence updating or installing the current version of Python is required across all these operating systems. Now, with a software package manager like Homebrew, installation, upgrade, and installation of packages of free and open-source software becomes much easier than the above process if you are using the operating system of mac operating systems. To install the latest version of python with pip package manager, the command to use is brew install python3. Package manager which any user, for instance, will use to install Python such as `apt-get` in Ubuntu-based systems or `dnf` in Fedora - installs Python in a way compatible with all else in the operating system. It must then be tried, installed and correctly placed. This is achieved through a command such as `python --version` or `python3 --version` in the terminal which would tell you that the correct version of Python is installed and available.

With writing and managing your code in Python, you will need to choose an Integrated Development Environment, or an IDE, or a text editor. IDEs enable you to add functionalities such as auto-completion, a debugger, and syntax coloring to your coding. Several popular IDEs have characteristics suitable to the development of Python, and most of these are unique in their offerings and vary greatly in complexity. There are popular IDEs for the development on the Python platform. PyCharm has free and paid editions - community, often referred to as a free version, and the professional version, respectively. PyCharm is a useful product since it provides a full set of tools to simplify the development of Python applications:

it provides intelligent code completion, project navigation, and integration with version control systems. It's really a great tool for web developers because of native support to the web frameworks Django and Flask.

Other than that, in terms of the user wanting lightweight or customizable alternatives, VS Code is a good option. VS Code originally started as a free, open-source text editor that has then morphed into the powerful tool it is today and with the implementation of extensions, it now will serve as a full-fledged IDE for Python. Once installed, it provides you with debugging tools, code linting, and the capability to run your Python scripts directly from the editor. It is flexible because it works with multiple languages and can be customized according to the exact needs of a developer because of its rich extension marketplace. Moreover, the high integration into Git as well as other version control systems makes it extremely popular among developers who function in collaborative environments. The other tool extremely widely used among Python developers is Jupyter Notebook specifically within data science and machine learning projects. Jupyter Notebook is a web application that enables writing Python code in an interactive format combined with code, visualizations, and narrative text all in one document. That is particularly useful in exploratory data analysis, where one can work through code in chunks and see how results come out right away, then tweak and repeat with ease. Jupyter is part of the larger Jupyter ecosystem, which also supports other languages, like R and Julia. This can be installed with reasonable ease using the `pip` package manager, or as part of the Anaconda distribution, which will give you a complete working environment with many tools specifically tailored toward the goal of data science.

With the IDE or text editor in place, managing packages and dependencies comes as a significant part of development environment setup. The native package manager for the Python module is called pip - Python Package Installer. Pip is usually used for installing and managing external libraries and frameworks that are not in the standard Python library. This is what I am looking at here: the pip command, which will allow you to install libraries that could expand Python into areas like data analysis, web development, and much scientific computing. For example, running `pip install numpy` from the command line would install the popular library for numerical computation. The installed packages are automatically manageable, updatable, or uninstallable if needed, and `pip` ensures that each package is compatible with the environment at hand. But then managing dependencies becomes important. For projects of higher complexities, this can be ensured with the right versions of libraries. This brings in virtual environments. A virtual environment is an isolated environment that contains its own installation of Python and libraries, independent of any global Python installation. This, therefore, ensures that each project can have varied dependencies without conflicts. For instance, one project could have a need for an older version of Django, while the other needs the latest version. Such projects can then exist on the same machine if both of them are to be using virtual environments.

This is actually quite straightforward, and you can use the package Python `venv` that comes with this version of Python to create a virtual environment. The command `python -m venv myenv` creates from any directory a new virtual environment in a directory called `myenv`. Once you have created an environment, you can activate it through operating system dependent commands. For instance, with macOS and Linux: `source myenv/bin/activate`, with Windows: `myenv\\\\\\ \Scripts\\\\\\ \activate`. Once the environment is activated, any libraries installed through pip are installed only within that environment, keeping the global Python environment clean while properly managing that project specific dependencies. And de-activating the virtual environment gets the user back into the global Python environment.

Besides library management, it most probably includes generation of a file called `requirements.txt`. The content includes all the project dependencies accompanied by versions of them. It's generated through the command `pip freeze > requirements.txt,` capturing all the libraries installed within the current environment along with their version. Then, the file may be shared with the other developers who would install all the libraries required for that project using the command `pip install -r requirements.txt`. That pattern can thus ensure uniformity of environments all through the development phase, most importantly in those environments that utilize collaborative work and even deployment to production systems. The environment configuration will be much better defined for the machine learning professional and the data scientist when using the Anaconda distribution. Anaconda is the Python Distribution along with a range of pre-installed data science libraries and tools such as Jupyter, NumPy, SciPy, and Matplotlib, among others. The `conda` package manager is also included with Anaconda. Unlike pip, the syntax of this command is used in a similar way. But unlike `pip`, however, packages that it works with are not only packages of Python but also packages which are not Python too, such as libraries written in C or C++. The very reason that makes it an extremely effective tool in the management of complex environments by the careful control of dependencies may well create potential conflicts. With Anaconda, developers can set up optimized environments fast for data analysis and machine learning jobs so that they can get on with the job without bothering with the headache of installing and configuring myriad libraries manually.

Besides setting the Python environment, by including version control in the workflow in the shape of Git, is another aspect that needs to be included in getting a development environment set up. Version control systems are of great importance for tracking changes in the code and collaboration between multiple different developers, along with a history of development in the project context. Git is the most widely-used version control system, and similar websites such as GitHub, GitLab, and Bitbucket provide cloud-based hosting for Git repositories. Git can be integrated with Python development so that developers would be working on various features or bug fixes in the development environment, then merge changes, and revert to earlier versions if needed. The built-in support of many IDEs for Git such as PyCharm and VS Code allow developers to commit code, push changes to remote repositories, and collaborate with other developers. With Git, you will be able to make use of continuous integration tools like Travis CI, Jenkins, or GitHub Actions and thus automate the testing and deployment of code. It makes it run test suites, check the quality of code, and deploy applications to production environments anytime in case of changes to the codebase. Configuring a CI pipeline will ensure that the code is trustworthy and of good quality, in particular as the projects scale to large and collaborative ones.

Finally, to any developer on a web application or service, setting up a local server or a containerized environment is often one of the typical required configurations. In this regard, Docker and similar tools allow shipping self-contained Python applications with their dependencies inside a container that can be run as consistently as possible across different environments. Its biggest use case is in the deployment of applications to production, as it would ensure the environment under which the code runs is akin to that in which it was developed. Docker also makes the development environment more streamlined;

any developer can use the same predefined configurations in Docker images. The setup of a Python environment can really be summarized into many steps from installation of Python itself to the final decision of which IDE will be chosen, how package management is to be implemented, how dependencies are to be handled, and what kind of version control will be necessary in order to make sure that development is efficient and reliable. Therefore, the flexible and roomy set of tools in Python accounts for such versatility in the needs of a project. Whether an application in web development, data analysis, or maybe something else - automating some task proper management with the help of virtual environments, integration with version control, lets developers create a Python environment on all levels of complexity in their project so that it works well for them. Well-configured environment forms one good basis for development. Instead of dealing with technical nightmares and having nightmares over configuration getting in the way, developers can focus more on writing code and solving problems.

Python Syntax and Basics

One of the most used programming languages in the market today is Python. This was because it was deemed easier to learn, versatile, and simple. Because of its characteristics, Python is a great language for beginning programmers and provides robust tools for more experienced developers as well. It is due to simple and intuitive syntax which liberates developers from being plagued by fear of getting lost in complex structures and lets them focus on solving problems. In order to write effective, maintainable, and readable programs, an understanding of the syntax and the basic idea of Python is then absolutely fundamental and forms the basis for further working with more complex projects within

Python. In this section, you will be learning the heart of Python grammar, ideas, and structures: variables, data types, control flow statements, functions, and error handling.

The main appeal of Python is its simplicity and readability. Python is quite insistent on writing clean and simple code that, quite often, reads like some kind of plain old English. Python is far easier to read because it uses indentation to define the code blocks instead of braces or other symbols, that are widely used in most other programming languages. Python uses indentation to define code chunks, including loops and conditionals, and even for function definitions to ensure that the code is readable and aesthetically consistent. For instance, this is how an `if` statement looks like in Python:

Print "x is greater than 10" if x is greater than 10, otherwise print "x is less than or equal to 10". The `print()` statements in this exercise are defined as a part of the `if` and `else` statements due to their indentation. Python will raise an `IndentationError} if there is inconsistent indentation. Python is much easier to read because of the use of indentation which also forces programmers to write clean, structured code right from the start. Any programming language must be aware of variables, and Python treats them in an easy-to-understand manner but still amenable to any and all adaptation. Variables in Python do not need to be declared neither should a specific type be assigned to them; rather variables are created through using the {=} operator to assign a value to them. Because Python is a dynamic language, the type of variable is determined by its assigned value at runtime. To make this clearer: {{{x = 10 y = "Hello, Python!" Z = 3.14 {▯<There, `z} is a floating-point value, `y} is a string, and `x} is an integer. Since Python is dynamically typed, a programmer can change the type of a variable simply by assigning a new value. Even though this flexibility is sometimes useful, it

also has the implication that, unless the developer catches such changes before running later parts of the code, errors will occur.

Python supports several basic data types, which is quite useful while building applications. These include booleans, strings, floats, and integers. Integers: They are just a collection of whole numbers. Floats: They have decimal points. Strings: Defined as characters when placed within a single or double quote. Strings are used for representing text. The logical values `True} and `False} are represented by Booleans. For example: a = 42; b = 3.14; c = "Python"; Float c; Character d = True # Boolean Other complex data structures designed to store groups of data, which include lists, tuples, sets, and dictionaries, also go under Python. Lists can be changed after they are created and are ordered. They are defined with the help of square brackets, and an index of an element is used to return a given element. For example: [1, 2, 3, 4, 5] is my_list. print([0] my_list) # Output: 1.

Like lists, tuples are ordered collections; but once created, their contents cannot be modified. Tuples are defined using parentheses: my_tuple = (10, 20, 30) Sets are defined using curly braces and collections of distinct elements in no specific order. They are useful for testing membership in a collection and for removing duplicates from a list: print(my_set) my_set = {1,2,3,4,4}. Curly braces are also used to declare dictionaries-sets of key-value pairs. Dictionaries are often used to keep linked data because every key in them is assigned a value. Keys are used for access to their corresponding values and should be unique: my_dict = {\\\"age\\\": 25, "name": "Alice"} Programmers need control flow statements as they allow the programmer to have control over the order in which their code gets executed. The most common standard control flow structures of the programming languages are supported by Python, including if statements, loops, and conditional expressions. Such statements as `if`, `elif`, and `else} are designed for running code blocks under predefined criteria. This would be the syntax for an `if} statement in Python: {{{x = 10 if x > 5: print(\\\"x is greater than 5\\") Print \\\"x is equal to 5\\\" if x == 5. print(\\\"x is less than 5\\"), otherwise.

In this example, the program determines if {x} is larger than 5, equal to 5, or less than 5, and then, depending on the outcome, executes the relevant block of code. Loops: A block of code can be run repeatedly using loops. Python supports both while and for loops. In order to iterate over a sequence, which can be a list, string, or any range of numbers, the `for` loop is used. For illustration purposes: for i in range(5), print(i). This code will print the numbers 0-4. The 'while' loop will run as long as some condition is True}. Suppose count = 0 and count < 5 print(count) count += 1. In this example, the while loop will run indefinitely until {count} equals 5. Python functions are basic building blocks that can encapsulate reusable code segments. Functions help programmers understand and read the code better by breaking down large programs into manageable sized pieces. For example, upon defining a function, one writes the keyword {def} followed by the function name and braces. The brace can include optional arguments to pass into the function. For instance, "Hello, {name}!" is printed by def greet(name): In this case, the function `greet` returns a greeting with a name if it is called with one argument `name}. Functions can also employ the `return` statement to return values. For example: def add(a, b): return add(3, 5) = a + b result print(outcome) # Outcome: 8"]] In the code below, the add function accepts two input parameters, {} and `b}, which are added up and returned. In the next step, the returned value is printed and assigned to the variable `result}.

Python also provides Lambda functions which are concise anonymous functions defined by using the `lambda` keyword. Lambda functions are very useful for simple, one-line operations that can be processed fast. Example Square = lambda x: x ** 2 print(square(4)) #Output: 16 \. When an error is encountered while executing a program, for instance, when it attempts to divide by zero or access an index of a list which does not exist, it raises an exception. The try block, the except block, and the finally block in Python enable the programmer to catch and handle the exceptional conditions. Code that may raise an exception is written inside the `try` block; if an exception is actually encountered, then it is caught and processed inside the `except` block. Code that should be executed regardless of whether or not an exception is thrown lives inside the {finally` block. Here is an example: {{{ try: result = 10 / 0 except ZeroDivisionError* print(\\\"Divide not possible by zero!\\\"). Final, print(\"This will always execute.\")\"}}END.

In this case, the software attempts to divide by zero, and it throws the error {ZeroDivisionError}. The except block catches the error and prints a message. Whether an error occurred or not, the finally` block of code is run. One of the reasons that Python is such a robust language is its support for object-oriented programming (OOP). The classes and objects supported by Python allow a programmer to describe how an object behaves and what properties it might have and mimic real-world entities. An object is an instance of a class, and a class is a blueprint for making objects. Methods are specified inside the class; classes are defined using the keyword `class`. Example: class Dog: def __init__(self, name, breed): breed = self.breed but not self.name print(f"{self.name} is barking!"); end def bark(self) my_dog = Dog("Golden Retriever", "Buddy") my_dog.bark() # Output: Buddy is yapping away! It has a class named `Dog` with a method called `bark` and two attributes: `name} and `breed}. This example shows an unique method to initialize an object once it's created: `__init__}. The `my_dog} variable invokes the `bark` method of the `Dog` class, which is an instance of the `Dog` class.

Python has a vast number of modules and packages as part of its standard library, with which one can easily carry out routine activity without having to start from the beginning of coding. The standard libraries include modules for managing dates and timings, working with files, communicating with the operating system, etc. For instance, the `datetime` module provides facilities for manipulating dates and times, and the `os` module provides functions that allow access to some system-specific variables and functions dealing with interaction with the operating system. As a demonstration: import datetime print(os.getcwd()) import os # Prints print(datetime.datetime.now()) the current working directory that is now open. # Prints the time and date as of now.

A rich third-party library and frameworks ecosystem fully extends the functionality beyond that of the standard library of Python. For example, if someone wants to develop web applications, they have powerful frameworks like Django and Flask; if they need to do some data manipulation and analysis, some of the most popular libraries are NumPy and Pandas. Because of these modules, Python is no longer a rigid language able to be used only for scientific computing, but it has become a truly workable language on a lot of different tasks-from direct use in web development to big comprehensive scientific computing. So, one who wants to be proficient with Python will need to know the basics and its syntax. As Python is feature-rich and varied yet shows due respect to readability, Python is the language in which many developers prefer, as it works in a lot of fields and is useful in creating clear, effective, and maintainable code from variables and data types through to control flow, functions, and error handling. This makes it an adaptive language for carrying out a lot of different sorts of programming projects, because large standard and third-party libraries are available. Understanding what the core of Python is all about can be great fun, especially if you don't have a significant background in programming.

CHAPTER II

Control Flow and Functions in Python

Conditionals and Loops

Conditionals and loops are the basic programming ideas related to control over the flow of execution of a program. Indeed, they were invented for making decisions and repeating operation, that would provide dynamic, flexible programs of good quality to the programmer. The Python constructs for these ideas are also transparent, easy to read, because this is compatible with the general simplicity of the language. This is important because it forms the basis of programming logic and, hence, allows one to develop complex behaviors for applications. For new as well as experienced programmers, what matters most is the skill in writing and using conditionals and loops, since it enables them to build complex behavior for applications.

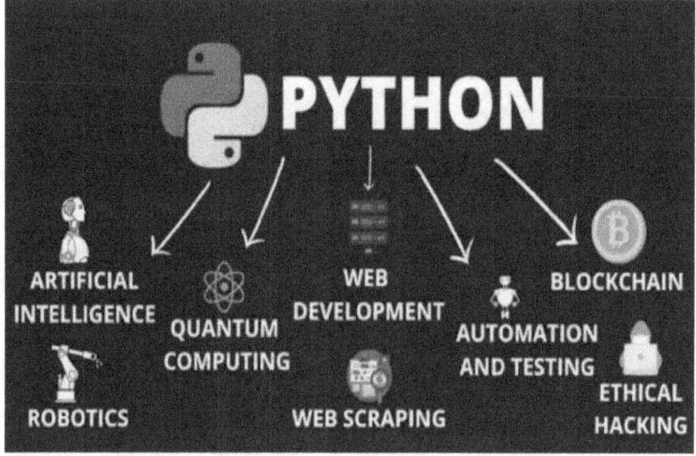

Conditionals are often referred to as branching statements. They are statements that allow a computer to follow different paths through multiple codes according to a given circumstance. They allow programmers to introduce judgment calls in their codes; for instance, a block of given code might run only if one condition is met. Conditionals are indeed essential in the creation of interactive programs and how they react to various inputs from users or other events. The three base constituents that build conditionals in Python are if, elif, and else. Statements evaluate expressions; the truth value of the expression dictates which of corresponding blocks of code to skip over or run. Probably the most elementary kind of conditional statement is the `if` statement, which allows the programmer to specify an expression to be tested; then, only if it is true will the block of code following this statement be executed. Provided there is another conditional, the program will go to the next one if the current one is false. If the above `if` statement evaluates to False, another condition is checked with the `elif` statement, short for "else if." It is thus possible for a program to have several pathways. Finally, if none of the conditions above are met, the `else` statement serves as a fallback and runs the block of code it is associated with. Because it generates branch logic, there can be more than one output depending on the arguments or variables.

Common application of conditional. It might be useful to compare data stored against the input credentials given by the user at login time. If these are matched-that is, given and stored password/username match-then access is granted. During such an event of unmatched credentials, several messages can be outputted to the user depending upon the application, stating that such a wrong login or password has occurred. Here, it uses conditionals and, what is more important, makes it work properly and allows the application's interaction, which would use a personalized feedback approach toward the input from the users. A neat encoding feature that allows a block of code to repeat is a loop. They are helpful for operations that have anything to do with iterations, like going through objects in a collection, repeating calculations many times, or gathering user input until some specified condition is met. There are two flavors of main kinds of loops available to you in Python: `for` loops and `while` loops. They do different, albeit slightly distinct things, and are suited for different contexts.

Repeat over an iterable-that is what the `for` loop does. That is the power to run a code block more than once so that each time through it can process a new element from some sequence. The `for` loop is useful if you know in advance how many iterations are going to occur. That is to say, the loop might be useful for looping over a list of things one at a time, then applying some transformation or just printing out each of them in turn. The `while` loop executes a block of code as long as some given condition is true. It is very handy where the number of iterations doesn't exist; rather, the number of iterations depend on some variables by the input given by the user or runtime values. For instance, a `while` loop could be used to repeatedly ask the user for input until he gives the proper data or himself wants to quit the usage of the software. Because loops are very flexible as far as repetitive operations are concerned, they are one of the most important elements of Python programming.

Loop control statements are the integral parts of loops. These statements make it possible for the programmer to step out of the normal loop iteration cycle. Two very commonly used loop control statements are "break" and "continue." In case the `break` statement is encountered while execution, it terminates the loop and execution proceeds to the next statement after that. That's very handy when the condition is satisfied, and there are no more iterations. For instance, while scanning, one can use a `break} statement for the purpose of omission of the loop and eventually stop execution whenever the sought value is located. The `continue` statement allows a loop to skip the remainder of the code in the current iteration and to proceed with execution with the next iteration directly. This one is handy if you need to execute a loop, even though some conditions will make its current iteration skip over. For example, imagine that you iterate over a list of numbers with a control structure, but you only want to work with the even ones. Then you can use `continue` to skip odd numbers.

With loops, conditionals are the forms of advanced programming logic. For instance, an application can pass over all of the inputs received by that user through a loop. While an invalid input exists, the same used iteration may be applied to validate the input and provide the proper feedback with conditionals as required. In summary, combining the features of conditionals with loops will provide a strong control mechanism for managing flow execution, which may be essentially unserviceable in the construction of robust and responsive programs to dynamic changes in inputs from users. The third characteristic of significant importance, which closely correlated well with conditionals and loops, has been error handling within the program. Programs frequently crash when other types of unforeseen circumstances occur- inputs are absent or runtime exceptions. This feature is implemented in Python, and errors are handled nicely and give developers the ability to code for recovery operations without affecting the flow of user experience. Developers can predict that the program may throw some errors that could likely occur and can define what the program should do when indeed an error occurs by using try-except blocks in conditionals and loops.

An example is where a developer using datatypes in application design can utilize error handling for identifying conditions under which the wrong datatypes or values are applied while reading user input in a loop. The program need not lose its direction when an error occurs but continue running in the case of a continued process in the case of a programmer who uses a try block to put the code interacting with the input. Applications require effective error handling to be able to steer a direction within an instance. Another thing, Python supports nested conditionals and loops, so programmers can structure complex iterative operations and decision making. Using nested conditionals, one may consider several conditions in a hierarchical order: one `if` statement is placed inside another `if}. Similarly, one can scan two dimensional data structure such as matrices or lists of lists by nesting it inside another loop. This nesting ability allows the programming logic to be written at a more fundamental level, and then harder problems can then be presented for solution.

In fact, conditionals and loops in Python are far more than decisions and repetition. They also make the realization of algorithms; such is the power that fuels the inside working of apps. Examples include search algorithms, sorting algorithms or data manipulation techniques whose efficient usage of conditions and loops are critical. It allows the programmer to structure the logic in these algorithms toward an effective solution for quite many computational problems. Other advanced features of Python are list comprehensions and generator expressions. Elements that bring a much more concise-written syntax to the creation of lists, besides iterating over data, compared with traditional conditionals and loops. They allow developers to create a list in one line of code, filter certain elements based on some condition, or change the values on the fly. Such a feature brings much brevity into the code, which makes it unusually legible and very effective. Another analogy, generator expressions also allow lazy evaluation, so that an iterator can build up only those values that are needed, which saves memory and, depending on the situation, provides better efficiency.

While this is good practice for any Python programmer to know how to use conditionals and loops, in practice there is a lot of practice needed to successfully master their effective use. Students learning a language are encouraged often to write small projects consisting of these structures and then, as they gain more experience with the concepts involved, systematically build up from there. Some examples of practical work that may drill the concept of conditionals and loops could include simple games, calculators, or data processing scripts. Basic software development is coding in such a way that it becomes readable and maintainable. Proper implementation of good practices while using conditionals and loops maximizes readability and maintainability of code: meaningful names to variables; comments left in places where complex reasoning is in order; and generally avoiding closely nested conditionals and loops as possible. Refactoring the code-making it less complex-simplifies it for future, perhaps wiser iterations of oneself and others to understand.

Loops and conditionals are good for more than one project. Code communication and documentation plays a very important role in the group development environment of software. Coding conventions and standards established when programming in a group ensure that there is one style to all, such that the code can be read more easily and reviewed each other's work. These will force the developers to improve their coding skills and develop reliable and efficient programs. Conditionals and loops are the two essential constructs in Python through which any programmer can develop nonrigid and dynamic applications. Conditionals perform operations, as devices for decision-making, by determining which path to take based on some conditions. Loops simply repeat actions; loops ensure data processing is more efficient. All these structures together let programmers take control of the flow in which a user interacts by making use of an algorithm that has some really complex logic. Even though highly, highly prevalent in many industries, Python is still basically a language. Hence, even getting familiar with conditionals and loops is still necessary for most individuals to become proficient with the language. Applications can be designed to be interactive and useful by the programmer himself if he is practicing how to use code standards and develops with his peers.

Functions and Scope

This is, then, the basic building block of code in programming: a function enables the reuse of sequences of the program. In Python, functions may be defined, passed as arguments and returned by others; thus, they stand first-class among the citizens of Python. Knowing how to construct and use functions is thus part of writing productive and maintainable code. This concept is so important that the visibility and lifetime of variables in a program are defined by scope, arguably at least as important a concept as functions. Therefore, this section will discuss the advanced concept of functions, starting with definitions, functionality, and how they ultimately dictate the behavior of programs.

A function is a code block that serves to do something. It takes parameters called arguments-the input. Output refers to the result when it is applied. The bit of code or a function could shatter the tough problems into smaller and manageable pieces for the ease of handling them. Modularity will support testing and debugging too while making code easy to understand. As a function may be invoked at several places of a program, encapsulation of code in functions prevents repetition and enforces Dryness'. A function in Python can be defined using the keyword `def`, including a name of the function, its parameters, all placed within parenthesis providing an explicit definition as to what kind of input the function is expecting. The code that gets executed when the function is called is found within the body of the function, which is defined using a colon once the parenthesis is closed. A `return` statement is often incorporated when defining functions that states what the function will yield and allows calling code to retrieve the result for further processing. However, not all functions must return a value; many may simply accept some arguments and perform computations without returning a result. One of the best features of functions is that they greatly make code reuse easier to do.

It is allowed to make more than one call to a function after declaration of the function and with different arguments. This avoids redundancy while making a change in the function at two different places, thus it makes code maintenance easier. Consider the example of the function that is aimed to calculate the area of a rectangle. It doesn't need to have different code for all the calculations because this function can be called with many different lengths and widths to calculate the areas of many different rectangles. It is also possible for functions to be composed with each other, so one function may call another. So, for example, we can say the simple building blocks of code which we might hope the language to describe as more complicated functionality. Thus, for example, if to abstract all computation into our own modules say a function that would tell us the area of a rectangle might call another function which tells us the perimeter,. It makes your code more readable and organizes better since the purpose of each function is clearer when viewed alone. One more feature of Python is you can call a function with fewer arguments than declared by allowing the concept of default parameters. The programmer can set up default values for parameters while declaring a function. Unless the caller supplies those parameters, the program uses the default values. This facility makes it easier to write code in places where some particular values are used in conventional practice but are seldom needed. It also permits more flexible calls of functions.

An important characteristic of Python functions is that they can accept a variable number of arguments. Such can be achieved by the `*args` and `**kwargs` syntax, which allows you to utilize functions that take any number of positional or keyword arguments, respectively. This means that you can build functions that are of a greater general-purpose in practice and which can serve for a broader variety of use situations. It really becomes very convenient when the number of input arguments in a function becomes changed. Besides functions, to be a good programmer, you must be aware of scope. Scope refers to the extent to which a variable is accessible or can be modified in the program. There is a Python rule defined by LEGB (Local, Enclosing, Global, Built-in) on how scopes work and how such variables will be resolved. This makes Python look first for a variable in the local scope then any enclosing scopes and then the global scope and finally the built-in scope. Local scope Variables defined by functions are said to be of local scope. All these local variables would actually be created during the time of function invocation and lie in a scope accessible only for use by the function itself. Immediately after the function has executed, these variables disappear, and it will raise an error if accessed from outside the function. This encapsulation can even further prevent unwanted interference between functions or in the global scope with variables defined inside other functions or even within the global scope. The term enclosing scope refers to the degree of enclosing functions; it proves particularly handy when discussing about nested functions .

When a function is declared inside another, the variables declared in the scope of the outer function are available to the inner function. Because the inner function is allowed to use and modify variables from its outer context, this attains more complex actions. This principle is particularly helpful when working with closures, where a function defined inside another function can be kept aware of that surrounding function's local variables even after that outer function returns. Variables declared at the top level of a script or module are global scope variables. Global variables can be accessed almost anywhere in the module; they can be accessed within functions. But as explained above, if you do use the `global` keyword then the global variable has to be declared modified from within a function. It makes explicit to Python that you really are using a global variable from outside the function rather than declaring a local variable of the same name. That's handy, though to be used sparingly so that one can avoid creating dependencies which make code harder to maintain and understand. Finally, built-in scope constitutes names which are always in scope. These include variables and functions, and among the latter are pre-defined functions which need no import statements. Here are `print() and `len. Therefore, the scope built into any standard programming language naturally includes all the most frequently used functions and constants and gives one the feeling of a standard library of easily accessible names, which makes the development process easier and more accessible. Subtleties of Scope Knowing how one can manage the lifetime and visibility of variables in a program are very important:.

Since erroneous scope handling would bring in possible unpredictable behavior and bugs into effects, one should take control with regard to where the variables are declared or how they are being used. For example, it could be that some global state is modified by one function in one place and not serviced afterwards. Then, some illusion crept into effects that might not have been thought of, primarily in larger codebases where many functions would expose the same global state. The ideas of functions and scope in Python make it pretty easy to write higher-order functions-that is, functions that take a function as an input or return one as a function. This paradigm also lets in strong abstraction as well as the reuse of the code. For example, a higher-order function may apply a function toward a set of values that come in as an argument, changing the list according to the function passed. This level of abstraction makes the code better expressed and can even promote functional programming, yielding usually well-maintainable, cleaner programs. Finally, Python supports lambda functions - anonymous functions declared by using the `lambda` keyword along with higher-order functions. Usually, they are used for momentary one-time operations that will not have an intention to be reused.

Sometimes it is very helpful to use lambda functions when a simple operation should be realized-for example, while one of the arguments should be a function passed to another function. The syntax of lambda functions is very short but one should use them carefully since, being applied thoughtlessly or overused, code may be less readable. In addition, a decorator is another very powerful feature of Python whereby you may also alter the behavior of a function or of a class. Hence, there is an absolute need to understand scope effects if you wish to employ a decorator. A decorator is a higher order function that lets a function extend some new functionality without altering the code where it is called, by passing it as an argument. It's often used in frameworks and libraries so that more than one function can consist of certain features which are normally applied to them, for instance, caching, authentication, and logging. As another example, one can log decorators, for example, that automatically apply to many functions so as to have their arguments or execution time logged: such a logging decorator provides useful information without explicitly including logging code in each method. Therefore, the structuring of code is improved and separation of concerns is promoted since decorator concerns the extra functionality independently of the logic in functions being decorated. They have plenty of advantages, but they will make programs harder specially with decorators, closures, and nested functions.

Hence, there must be a way of striking the right balance between making use of these powerful features and code readability by developers. Considering these possible threats of complexity, one can still advantageously utilize modularity and abstraction in functions through proper design, based on norms for naming conventions and proper documentation. Even interactions between functions and scope can affect procedures for debugging and testing. Functions significantly aid the ability of developers to step off specific functional components of their program; it aids them in unit testing because they control the scope of variables in encapsulating behavior. Every function can be tested independently for it to be sure that it acts as expected under any given circumstance. Isolation also makes it quicker to identify and debug the problem because nothing else in the code will interfere with a function's ability to trace back failures to either its inputs or internal logic. Apart from unit testing, the knowledge of scope is required when variable-related problems come under debugging. Variable shadowing can occur when a local variable shadows the wrong global variable with the same name thus causing problems of scope. It is quicker for a developer to know and debug variable visibility lifetime-related issues, which can benefit the programmer ending up with code much more dependable and stable. Robust Python applications rely on function and scope when implementing numerous evolving programming techniques.

Thirdly, these concepts are all the more relevant with the advent of burgeoning functional programming paradigms that nurture styles of writing code that is high in quality and maintainable. With the use of decorators, higher order functions, and controlled scope the scientists would be able to write robust elegant and evocative code. In a nutshell, what really Python programmers need, that is the basic building blocks-the basic elements of a function and scope-presented to programmers in efficient organization of their code. Logic encapsulation is what gives a function, encouraging code reuse whereas scope refers to how long variables are visible and how long a program lasts. It is within this mix of the two that one finds a program design method which is dynamic and flexible enough to meet many requirements. It is in finding a middle ground where the strength of functions can be brought to bear without the code becoming unreadable that the challenge to the developer lies. While working out the niceties of functions and scope, careful design with rigorous testing can make all the difference in helping developers get the most use out of features and scope as possible to bring about scalable high-quality software. A proper grasp of these very basic concepts would be invaluable to any serious programmer hoping to make it in Python and beyond.

Error Handling and Exceptions

This is because exception handling or error handling elements of the program make the applications robust and reliable. However, most times, during the development process, unexpected events run along with network problems, resource constraints, or even mistakes by users. The program may then fail with results that provide a poor user experience as well as large losses in data, if proper error handling is not incorporated. Python makes exceptions structured ways to deal with failures where the programmer can foresee potential problems and properly throw solutions. It is important to know how to address exceptions and failures in the implementation of robust and well-supported software.

In general, any event that takes place during the execution course of a program that interferes with a program's normal sequence of instructions is generally known as an exception. Python raises an exception when an error occurs, so you can trap that and thereby prevent your program from abruptly terminating. A number of events will raise an exception, including trying to divide by zero, gaining access to a file that does not exist, or trying to use an index that is actually beyond the bounds of a list. When an exception has happened and therefore interrupted the normal running of the program, Python looks for an exceptional handler that exactly matches the error. Python uses a framework called "try-except" blocks to control errors. The code that is in the `try` block is that which may raise an exception. If an exception happens in this block, it moves the control to the block that corresponds to the `except` block so the error may now be nicely handled. Such a construct makes the handling of errors more meaningful and organized because programmers can specify which actions should be taken in response to the different types of exceptions.

Consider how a program would attempt to read data from a file for example. If the file was not found when trying to open it, then a `FileNotFoundError} will be raised. The program can give feedback to the user without crashing by encapsulating the code in a `try` block for opening the file and an appropriate `except` block for catching this special error. It can be returned back as a response by querying the name of another file to input, or by telling him that he cannot access that file. Python can catch any exception which might be raised in a single generic `except block; but it should be used very judiciously. It is just going to hide the problems which really need to be exposed. Generally, it is best practice to catch individual exceptions wherever possible, so that errors are possibly better handled and the context of what went wrong is clearer.

Besides that, there is an opportunity to use an `else` block in the framework of exception handling; such a block will be executed only in case when the block of `try` will not throw any exceptions. It can be handy for code that should run only when the code before it ended correctly. Finally, Python supports a `finally` block, which is always executed, with or without some exception occurred. This is especially useful for resource cleanup, like flushing files or deallocating network connections, since it ensures clean-up operations occur even if an exception was raised. Although the control structure implemented by `try-except` is foundational for exception handling, it is equally important to recognize the fact that there exist many types of exceptions which could be raised. Python comes with many in-built exceptions, each involving a different form of failure. Among the most frequently occurring inbuilt exceptions are `TypeError`, `ValueError`, `IndexError`, `KeyError`, and `ZeroDivisionError`. These in-built exceptions are of great importance for making error handling more efficient. It allows the programmer to predict the likely problems and takes remedial action at the right moment. Python also enables developers to create new user-defined exceptions. A new class to define an exception is made using inheritance from the base `Exception` class. This is useful where developers need to add more meaning and clarity to an application by writing exceptions based on the specific requirement of an application.

For example, a function intended to read user input that is supposed to follow some criteria, may come up with a programmer's custom exception to raise when the input fails to act according to those criteria. Instead of returning a general message to a user, a developer can actually return useful information to the user about what went wrong by throwing a custom exception. This improves the user-friendliness of the method by offering more clues about how to solve a problem. The main element of the Python error handling mechanism is intentional exception throwing. A developer might use the {raise` statement to manually throw an exception, enforcing a constraint or to indicate something hasn't been done. For example, when a function has been passed an invalid argument it may raise a `ValueError` back to the caller as a reminder that input does not meet any one of a set of predetermined standards. Developers can make their error messages more informative and assist in troubleshooting by raising exceptions deliberately.

In addition to that, an exception caught by raise statement can be used to raise again; this opens an opportunity to handle or log before letting an error propagate up the call stack. This is very useful in those scenarios where the exception is relevant further up in the chain of execution but one step of handling needs to be done. Beside catching and resolving exceptions, error handling and exception management involve debugging and logging. To help diagnose and repair, it should be important to record pertinent error information at the time of an exception. Python's `logging` module can be used to record the error messages, stack traces, and other pertinent information to a file or console. All such data would result in understanding user behavior, knowing the trends in failures, and hence improving the overall reliability of the application as a whole.

For instance, imagine a Web application crashing each time or almost every time it tries to access the database. When bad things do happen, engineers know more about the conditions in which those bad things occur and can more precisely identify and correct the causes of failures by keeping detailed error messages and stack traces. Good logging techniques are composed out of a history record of problems and solution that will improve the maintainability of the application and assisting the debugging process. An error-handling design can really enhance maintainability in the long term and does not deter from a good user experience. Standard error-handling procedures allow developers to develop applications that are the most unwaveringly resistant to unexpected occurrences. In other words, it means stating steps and methods on how exceptions should be handled, noting any form of exception a function may cause, and making sure that the error message is clear and informative.

Error handling is a very nice weapon, but it should never be regarded as a substitute for writing clean, robust code and must therefore be remembered. Actually, the goal of the developer is to foresee any potential issues and eliminate them with robust design and verification. For instance, checking user input before you do some further processing on it may help in avoiding most common exceptions beforehand. Active programming practices applied in combination with error handling lead to applications that work well and are a delight to use. Error handling is especially important in terms of testing. Most testing frameworks for automated testing contain testing of the error handling code so that exceptions get raised appropriately and also handled correctly. Unit tests may be written to determine whether a certain exception gets thrown under specific conditions. This establishes the fact that the logic of error handling is correct. Added above the quality improvement of code is error handling and testing, which gives a sense of confidence to the users about its dependability.

By summarizing the above points, the developer can confirm the possibility of some code containing a defect by writing a unit test about checking if a function throws a `ValueError` when given some erroneous input. In this manner, testing for expected behaviors in error cases would avoid the potential failure on deploying into a production environment while lessening the likelihood that there could be critical issues arising during runtime. Beyond documenting what the code is meant to do, these tests can also help in a teaching process of letting other developers precisely how the system ought to react when presented with some information. With apps of increasing complexity comes a good level of efficient error handling and exception management. There are probably much bigger sites of failure that come into play when you work with databases, or web services, and so on, which you then have to account for. In order to handle events elegantly, you would very often be required to have strong error-handling methods in place in scenarios involving network errors due to timeouts or connectivity issues, for example. Long before such problems may occur, developers can specify the right mechanisms for providing error handling. Developers could very well work out applications that can continue to work and respond even in the presence of problems.

Exceptions also require special care in asynchronized programming, such as using Python's `asyncio` module. How that problems in one coroutine cannot immediately come about in another makes asynchronous code difficult with regard to exception propagation. In an asynchronous code, developers mostly handle exceptions by using some techniques such as `asyncio.gather()` with proper error-handling techniques in every coroutine. It will guarantee all possible exceptions are caught and handled correctly while execution for better analysis of possible problems that may arise. This design philosophy indicates overall quality of application as well as a technical concern with the handling of errors. This attention to error management reflects an interest in the applications being dependable and user-friendly. When things have not gone right, it is really important to give the consumer very pithy, useful feedback so he or she can move from muddle and irritation to some solution. That user-centered approach toward error management might improve the overall usability of an application just a lot.

For instance, if the form fails submitting when the application comes across validation errors, a good application should be able to print an error message indicating which fields one has to correct. Beyond assisting in the resolution of an error clearly on the user's end, it gets established with the user and induces a factor of trust in its ability. For such mission-critical applications, error management would really be quite critical. It may range from banking software to the medical software. Untreated exceptions in these fields lead to pretty serious consequences, such as wrong calculations, losing data, and even risking human life. Therefore, the developers working on these categories should also prioritize error management and testing first, so that these applications could either meet or withstand any new condition and work properly.

As software grows and becomes more complex, error handling can become much more challenging. Exceptions over numerous modules, libraries, or services calls do demand good planning and forethought. A central logging system as well as a standard approach to error handling makes it easier and also allows system components to more easily harmonize their approach on how errors should be handled. For instance, a web application can make the handling of many routes and controllers' errors easier by having a middleware component catch and handle exceptions in one place. This reduces duplicate code and also provides for an uniform user experience of errors—wherever throughout the application they may occur. New paradigms and new methodologies in software development have a huge influence on approaches toward error handling. Actually, as soon as microservices design came, the error treatment became extremely problematic for developers in the case of remote systems. Developers have to introduce mechanisms for managing their mistakes while crossing boundaries between different services since failure can occur at any level of the service chain. One of the few generally applicable techniques to design for resilience is the combination of ensuring that, at a higher abstraction level, the system can recover from transient failures by implementing fallback mechanisms, retries, and circuit breakers.

With applications of artificial intelligence and its offshoot, called machine learning, error handling is more complex. Developers need to remember that, with models of ever-increasing complexity and driven by data, there are probability possibilities of errors either in data processing or the model prediction itself. In this type of situation, well-defined error handling processes must be in place to keep the system intact and produce results. In a nutshell, the basic features of Python programming related to exceptions and error handling allow a programmer to handle the unforeseen state of runtime anomalies and provide solid software. Developers can turn to the error management along with improving the code robustness due to the logging techniques, forced exceptions, and usage of the `try-except` mechanism. Knowing standard exceptions and creating one's own variations when needed allow developers to elegantly handle specific fault conditions. Apart from this, the user-centered approach toward error handling as well as the integration of error handling with testing processes enhances the quality of software systems.

Since Python emerged as one of the leading programming languages in various domains, professionals holding jobs related to application development should be familiar with error handling and exceptions. A good developer can predict problems, implement proper techniques for error handling and inform the users about meaningful feedback. Based on the concepts of error handling and exceptions, software developers can create the best software meeting their functional requirement at the same time offering a better degree of reliability and wonderful experience to the users. In the ever-changing world of software, robust error handling is of extreme importance because it offers developers the very building blocks of making long-lived, high-quality programs.

In short, every Python programmer needs to be taught the art of error handling. More than simply catching exceptions, it is actually a manifestation of a better overall context of user interaction and program behavior. The more complex software is going to prove to be, the more error handling will matter. It should therefore be the intention of developers to come up with a system that is not only useful but also able to graciously handle failures when they occur by providing flawless experience even to a user facing unforeseen difficulty. So, with error handling, one may establish a good foundation by which developers can move with the frustrations that accompany new software development while maintaining robustness, dependability, and user friendliness of their programs.

CHAPTER III

Working with Data Structures

Lists, Tuples, and Sets

Python is highly known for its ease of use and flexibility in handling various types of data structures. Among the wide types of collections in Python, the traditional three most important collections that people have used for a long time are lists, tuples, and sets. There are three kinds of data structures that exist for use under various scenarios, but each of them has its own purpose. Since most algorithms and applications revolve around these data structures, it is very important that every Python programmer learn to use them correctly.

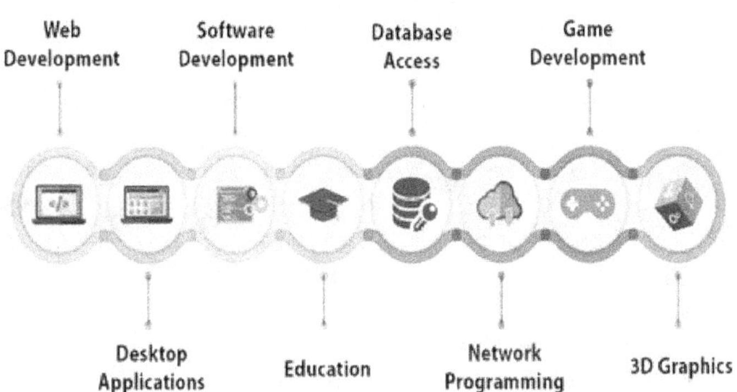

The most commonly used data structure in Python is a list. They are mutable; that is, once a list has been defined, elements in the list can be changed. Lists can contain many different objects, including text, numbers, or even other lists filled with many types of data. This is what makes lists so dynamic and able to hold large collections of data. Lists are declared in square brackets and elements inside it by a comma: For example, if you would like to write a list, you would input:. All of use, from simple data storage to the complex applications of data processing, may come alive through lists thanks to their elasticity. However, the strongest characteristic feature would be that lists possess procedures inside themselves which render easy manipulation of the data: such as adding items through `append()` and `extend()`, deleting them through `remove()}` and `pop()`, and accessing the different elements through indexing. Lists prove really useful when you only want to access-a slice of the list and just want to draw out a part of the list. This is primarily useful if only part of the data needs processing. Here's an example in respect of listing: `my_list[:3]` returns `[1, 2, 3]`, which just so happens to be the first three elements in the list if sliced up by listing. The other very important feature is that lists remember natural order. This feature is very helpful in processing an array of user entries or maintaining a neat collection of tasks sometimes when the order of data matters. Besides that, lists permit duplicate elements so that developers can place nonunique values without any limitation imposed by limiting constraints.

However, despite all these benefits with the usage of lists, they have some performance limitations. The size of the list itself-change in terms of adding and removing entries-can be expensive concerning performance because they are mutable, especially huge lists that would mean scaling may yield more complicated processing times. Lists also consume more memory as compared to other data structures because they carry extra overhead for dynamic resizing. Tuples are generally different from lists in terms of mutability, yet they store their data similarly. In the case of a tuple, the elements cannot be modified once created so cannot themselves be changed and, therefore, are immutable. This is useful where it needs to retain its data integrity and does not need to be updated for this reason. Tuples are defined using parentheses, and elements are separated by commas. Here's an example code:. The most important advantages of tuples: they are faster to generate than lists. Because tuples are immutable, they cannot be changed; so, they consume memory much better than lists. Because they cannot be changed, they make excellent keys for dictionaries; this is why they are such excellent hashable types of data. This is very useful for the purpose of establishing links or mappings between key-value pairs.

Lists also support slicing and indexing. Any assignment to a tuple would raise a TypeError since they are immutable. Tuples can be used for storing data that should not change at runtime since they are immutable. Tuples can be used for example to represent fixed data structures such as RGB color values, coordinates or any other type of data that should not change. This makes the data structure much more flexible with the fact that it can make nested tuples. Developers can represent multi-dimensional data by nesting tuples inside other tuples to enable them to represent very complex data structures. For instance, python point_3d = (x, y, z) defines a tuple that represents a point in three-dimensional space. Tuples do have their advantages and disadvantages. Among those disadvantages is its lack of a comprehensive collection of built-in data manipulation capabilities, which is one big disadvantage similar to lists. For example, there are ways for adding or removing elements in a tuple that should be done dynamically.

The third most basic data type in Python, sets, also offers another special method for organizing data sets. Sets are unordered, unique collections that can't contain duplicate values. The property of the sets makes them extremely useful for uniqueness operations, membership tests, and mathematical set operations. A set can be declared using `set()` or by curly braces: `my_set = {1, 2, 3, "Python",

4.5}. Another important advantage of sets is that they are very efficient in testing membership. Use of hash tables implemented inside the sets makes testing membership much more efficient than for lists or tuples. For example, if you have the case where you would have to remove duplicates from a list, or you are processing a large dataset where items must be unique, then the best candidate is a set in terms of requirements. Other operations of sets include union, intersection, difference, and symmetric difference. For instance, you can calculate an intersection of two sets either using the {&} operator or the `intersection()` method. Doing so allows the developers then to better deal with complex work jobs pertaining to data process and analysis. Finally, the sets will represent the relations among the different datasets, thereby opening entirely new possibilities for additional types of data manipulation and analysis methods.

Even though sets hold all these advantages, they do not lack disadvantages. Sets cannot be indexed nor sliced since they are nondeterministic. Thus, their elements cannot be accessed directly through their positions. It may thus prove fatal on operations whose order is of significance on data processing for a feature like such to be detrimental. On the second aspect, since set elements can only be accepted to have hashable contents, they cannot support changeable data types, say lists or dictionaries. This will depend on the particular application requirements weighed against the properties of each data structure whether lists, tuples or sets are better suited for the problem. Apps where data is supposed to change a lot should use lists; element order is important. Tuples are best used for holding immutable collections of data; data does not change during runtime of an application. A set would suffice in tasks that require membership testing to be efficient and uniqueness. For example, if one wanted to log the various multiple input values coming from different users, then a list will suffice to log that information. On the other hand, a tuple would be appropriately used when one wants to keep in memory an array of some constant set, such as color values in RGB. It would have been a set if the function removed or eliminated duplicate values from the collection because it had efficient operations on retaining only unique values.

Another significant issue is performance. The lists are very useful, but they consume many resources in big collections with dynamic scaling. Because tuples are immutable, they provide better memory and access times; therefore, they must be used whenever strict data integrity can't be compromised. Sets are useful to data analysis applications because it supports mathematical operation, and testing in them for membership is the fastest. That is also made more efficient, because of the library of Python functions and methods available for one to use. For example, to get the size of a list, tuple, or set, one can make use of the len() functions. If fast membership testing for elements of lists, tuples, or sets is needed then the `in} keyword would be enough. These are built-in capabilities in Python that may ease common data management actions made much easier. Lists, tuples, and sets offer some really powerful features and applications besides their obvious functionality, making them widely useful in many programming contexts. For instance, lists support list comprehensions that is, on an existing list, concise means of building a new list by applying an expression to each element in the list. The very useful function allows the developer to write clearer and, above all, more readable code. For example, a list comprehension would look as follows: sqrt_numbers in Python = [x ** 2 for x in range(10)] .

Consequently, what would be calculated is a list of squares of numbers from 0 up to 9. It can also be applied more flexibly when you make use of conditional statements, with the help of list comprehensions filtering your data. Tuples allow unpacking: the assignment for several variables from a tuple can be done in one go. That comes pretty handy when working with functions that return multiple values. This exercise gives you an example of where you would unscramble the return values into different variables, say, if you think that a function returns a tuple of results. Python def calculate(a,b): calculate(10, 5) return a+b,a-b sum_result, difference_result Here, the function `calculate` returns a tuple containing both sum and difference values for two numbers, unpacked into separate variables, and further used:. Sets provide robust set operations that are incredibly useful for all kinds of data analysis tasks. The method `difference()` can return the elements that are in one set but not in another. In case you need to merge sets, there are both `union()` method and the `|}` operator. All of these operations might become useful during data processing: filtering or datasets merges or finding common items between several collections.

Sets are used more broadly in statistical analysis, and of course, even in graph algorithms, and for cleaning. For example, the developer might use a set to find and delete the duplicate items in some source of customer records obtained through some sort of data cleaning, thereby improving the quality of the data enormously for further processing or analysis. Sets, tuples, and lists represent some of the most elementary structures in Python. These appear to be different yet unique structures that make the sets, tuples, and lists accessible structures in helping achieve the required uses and functions applied in effective management of data. Lists are highly appropriate for various applications since they provide flexible collections offering dynamic data storage and handling. Tuples are very good for the storage of fixed sizes of data because it is more performance-efficient and provides immutability. Use of sets in data-intensive processes mainly because it offers unique collections that are unordered excellently, well for mathematical operations, and membership checking.

From the above descriptions, to design reliable and efficient applications, every Python developer should be knowledgeable about the properties and advantages of each one of these data structures in order to assure both reliability as well as the successful applications. An appropriate choice of data structure maximizes efficiency and increases code readability of developers in accordance with a requirement set of their applications and the integrity of data. It has to be known because the programming language is still in its developing stages. With all of this, programming in Python will always make use of lists, tuples, and sets to properly create efficient software solutions that can adapt to a rapidly changing world of technology, whether for simple scripts or complex applications. Then, data structures can further be used by the developers as a source of opening new channels for handling, analyzing and administering data through efficient planning and execution of designs. These bring their projects and applications at a successful generation in the end.

Dictionaries and Hashmap

Among all the data used in programming, data structures play a very important role in organizing information, storing, and retrieving it. In such a context, the dictionary or hash map is the most useful and versatile, and especially when applied in Python. Indeed, dictionaries, which are built-in Python data structures, rely on a system of data stored in pairs of values and keys, while hash maps are usually considered as the underlying technology that ensures fast retrieval of data. This section presents some of the characteristics, functionalities, and practical uses of Python dictionaries and hash maps, which will display the application and feasibility of the concepts in software development.

A dictionary is a collection of unordered objects that can be modified. In Python, keys of a dictionary must be strings, numbers or tuples because they must be unique, but immutable. Values may be any type of data, even lists or other dictionaries. This makes dictionaries useful for holding complex structures of data-of course, this is also why they're such a great resource for engineers. Curly Brackets {{}} A dictionary is defined with curly brackets {{}}. Key - value pairs are separated by a comma, using colons for pairs. Example of an elementary dictionary: As illustrated in the above example, keys are { "name", { "age", and { "city" while corresponding values are { "Alice", {30, and { "New York". Such an organization of data allows easy data manipulation, access, and modification. The main reason why dictionaries are useful is that information can be retrieved quickly from a dictionary. Since a dictionary in Python is realized as a hash table, the hashing algorithm maps each one of the dictionary's keys to a unique index. As dictionaries allow lookup and insertion in time complexity to be $O(1)$ on average, they are among the handiest instruments for the organization of large databases. This feature is crucial where rapid data access is a pre-requisite-such as in applications pertaining to web development and data processing activities. Although Python dictionaries are very intuitive and even to create, they are basically founded on hash map concepts. Hash map is a data structure that has the capability of mapping keys to their respective values using a hash function. Therefore, when a new key was added to the hash map, the index based on the key would be used by the hash function to actually put an appropriate value into an array, giving you immediate access to the value correlated with the key.

It's the most important concept which describes how hash maps work: a good hash function spreads keys as uniformly as possible to the indices, so it is much less likely to have collisions-multiple keys mapping into the same index. Hash maps apply techniques of resolution by open addressing or chaining, where several elements are stored at the same index. Python's dictionary management happens such that, with a dynamic array of storage, it auto-increases in size as elements are added. How that works, its ability to maintain efficiency during resizing, and its average-case time complexity staying constant while growing is what keeps this data structure constant. Its worst-case scenario is O(n) but does occur in collision-intensive or during heavy resizing operations, though the average-case performance is O(1). However, this Python dictionary is very often one of the most effective data structures because of what was ultimately designed into them to avoid those risks. Python dictionaries contain many built-in methods that make manipulation of data very easy. Because of the availability of several such methods, using dictionaries is far more flexible and convenient, and they form a premium item in the toolkit of the Python coder. Some of the most generally used dictionary methods are shown below: The keys corresponding to the accessible values can be indexed to access the latter. This would return {Alice}. End. A new key with a value will assign, adding the key-value pairs or the new key-value pairs to the dictionary. `my_dict["email"] = "alice@example.com"`, for example, creates an email under a new key called "email.". The value can be assigned or overwritten by accessing the values by their keys. `{my_dict["age"] = 31}`, for example, updates Alice's age. Deleting key-value pairs: Dictionaries can delete key-value pairs using the `del` statement. To delete the entry for { "city" }, for example, use {del my_dict["city"]}.

Loops can be used to write the enumeration of keys into a list so that all values, all keys, or all items can be looped over. For example, using my_dict.items() as the basis, the following will print in Python: print(f" {key}: {value}") Getting keys and values: This method returns lists of the dictionary's keys and values for `keys()` and `values()`, respectively. Now developers can readily access all the keys or values. Testing whether a key is in a dictionary can be accomplished using the `in` keyword, which gives an efficient way of testing for data. Merging Lexicographies The `|}` operator is a recent addition to Python 3.9 so now the merging of a dictionary becomes a very simple task. For example, in using `new_dict = my_dict | another_dict}`, we get the new resulting dictionary with the merged key-value pairs. The above methods and many more make dictionaries versatile, so one can handle data very efficiently in different applications. Dictionaries in Python are highly useful in many real-world applications across different domains and scenarios. For example, the data from a JSON file or even an API is usually in key-value-pair form and thus very easily can be stored inside dictionaries; extraction and further manipulation of data becomes very easy for further analysis. They can also be applied when implementing data models, for instance. A dictionary would represent a user profile in an application - the web, for instance. Within such an application, the key-value pairs can hold different kinds of user data like name, email, and so on preferences. User data could easily be managed, attributes could readily be updated, and information could effectively be accessed.

It relies heavily upon dictionaries. Where retrieval is expensive, there might be dictionaries where retrieved data is stored. This way, retrieval occurs much faster without having to dip into repeated computation or searching at the database level. This is very useful with web applications in which speed becomes an indispensable component. The usage of the dictionary is very natural in counting and frequency analysis. It can be further extended for summarization of data by quantifying the frequency of each word while scanning a text document. A simple loop that iterates over the words of the text and updates the count of every word that appears in the dictionary is often used in achieving this. Another good application of graph structure representation is in an adjacency list form wherein each key maps to a node and the value associated with it forms a list of neighboring nodes. Graph algorithms could make use of this representation where dictionaries are being used; thus, making graph traversal and manipulation efficient for programmers to use techniques like depth-first search and breadth-first search. Of course, along with all of the above marvelous abilities, this involves its own range of restrictions and limitations. Mainly that dictionary keys must be immutable. That makes it sometimes inflexible for certain applications because data types like a list or other dictionaries cannot be used as a key. The developers need to carefully decide what to use in order for the developed keys to meet the criterion.

Another thing to keep in mind is dictionaries happen to be a good bit more of a memory-intensive data structure than something like lists or tuples. That could result in increased memory usage simply on account of overhead from hashing the table in-place and managing collisions; not particularly germane to memory-sensitive designs but note it anyway. For example, Python dictionaries have average-case time complexity as O(1) for operations, but big resizing or collisions could severely degrade worst-case performance. If heavy dictionary utilization is part of building systems, developers should then be very careful, especially when applications need serious efficiency. The other is that an iteration over the keys does not necessarily imply an iteration over the entries in the order they were made, since dictionaries are intrinsically unordered-that may be damaging if the order is meaningful in the data. Python 3.7 and up preserve the insertion order as an implementation detail for dictionaries; earlier versions should not be relied upon to do so. Such a large number of advance features makes Python dictionaries significantly more useful that accompany them. One of such features is dictionary comprehensions, which enables developers to build new dictionaries from already existing iterables as rapidly and comfortably as possible. For instance, one might create a dictionary pairing integer values with their squares: Squared_dict in Python = {x: x**2 for x in range(10). Because of this, generating dictionaries is easier and more efficient, and cleaner code results in less explicit looping.

One can nest dictionaries, and so one can have quite complex data structures. A way to write nested data is by using dictionaries that also store other dictionaries as values. This form is especially useful whenever one needs to configure an application or whenever the relations between data are significant: Because of this layering functionality, it is, therefore easy to arrange relevant information so that management and access to configuration settings are made easier. Another module included in Python is `collections,` which contains special dictionary-like structures: `defaultdict`, `OrderedDict,` etc. Since the nonexistent keys can have a default value, a so called `defaultdict` simplifies the code otherwise requiring explicit checks for the existence of keys. On the other hand, an {OrderedDict} guarantees constant iteration order since it is ordered according to the order keys appear in this structure. The basic data structures provided by Python, allowing the most effective and adaptable means of dealing with key-value pairs, are dictionaries, hash maps. That is why, due to the outstanding retrieval and manipulation performance, dictionaries implemented by Python as hash maps have become an extremely useful tool for developers and development teams working in various fields. Thus, dictionaries manifest themselves as very effective tools in the hands of developers, bursting with wide-scope capabilities and excellent applications in practice. These can be traced at the administration of complex data structures and the resolution of a wide range of programming tasks.

Dictionary usage has proven to be extremely helpful during the development of modern software. Some of that evidence are data to web development techniques and caching. Demanding good data management, the future of any Python developer will be all the more upon usage with dictionaries and hash maps. The mastery of this piece of art will effectively make it easy to enhance the performance, optimize codes, and build reliable systems in accordance with the set expectations in this now data-driven environment. Dictionaries and hash map make a larger role in such an increasingly complex environment of programming. These data structures will greatly impact the future directions of programming if programmers continue to build complex applications and process large amounts of data. The dictionary and hash map functions will form the basis of the Python programming environment for a simple job or algorithms with complexities. In this manner, this shall give programmers an effective, structured, and efficient solution for problems in the modern world.

Advanced Data Manipulation Techniques

Because it enables data scientists and programmers to effectively clean, convert, and analyze data, data manipulation is an important component of both data science and programming. Data manipulation often involves performing a number of complex operations on vast amounts of data-things that would be impossible without the strong ecosystem of libraries and tools that Python supports. In this lesson, you will learn some advanced techniques for manipulating data using Python with a focus on libraries that provide strong abilities to handle data, such as NumPy, Pandas, and others. Data manipulation refers to processing, transformation, or alteration of data to provide it with the form or shape needed. It encompasses various activities, such as data cleaning, transformation according to an analysis design, aggregation for reports, and reshaping according to certain needs. An effective system of data manipulation would have developers and analysts come to new insights from the data in turn, thus improving upon decision-making and outcomes.

Python is very popular in the data manipulation space mainly due to ease of use and powerful tools. Of these, the key framework for manipulating and analyzing the data was Pandas, which provided data structures like Series and DataFrame, which made structured data easier to manipulate. On the other hand, NumPy does great with big arrays and matrices and is of paramount importance when it comes to numerical computations. Mastering complex Python data manipulation techniques is, therefore, important to data professionals as demand about data-driven decision-making increases. Deep methods in this section will include data wrangling, filtering and selection, aggregation, reshaping, missing values handling, data combining, and sophisticated transformations.

Data Wrangling is a key process in data manipulation, or merely cleaning and converting raw data into an appropriate format for use. This kind of work recommends Pandas as it possesses strong data structures and functions. Handling mismatched data type, column renaming, transformation are some examples of data wrangling. Handling mixed data types is quite a common pain in wrangling. For example, a column in a DataFrame could hold strings and numbers-meaning they would cause issues if not represented properly. Pandas' package includes functions, `pd.to_numeric()` and `pd.to_datetime()`, that convert columns to appropriate types automatically. Such functions also include ways for users to decide how non-convertible values are treated, so mistakes are processed gracefully. Rename columns is the other useful data wrangling process. More descriptive column names have added readability to the code, but also to the data itself. Rename columns in Pandas can be done through the `rename()` method either using `columns` option or/and with a dictionary of old-new names assignment. The example code would be as follows: ```python df.rename(columns={'old name': 'new_name'}, inplace=True)>/>.

Apart from column renaming, data format conversion is a very common requirement, especially in date and time-related columns. Date textual representations can easily be converted to `datetime` objects using rich parsing and formatting capabilities available in Pandas. This is essentially a pre-requisite for any kind of date differencing or time-series analysis. The step following the organization of data into some form that works is data filtering and selecting relevant data to analyze. Good indexing features offered by Pandas make filtering very easy: specifically, by criteria. Boolean indexing is probably one of the most used methods for selecting data. Suppose you wanted to analyze sales data stored in a DataFrame and you wished to filter rows where the sold amount exceeded a certain level. You would simply write the following simple boolean expression: Panda's has boolean indexing and the `query()` method. This makes using text expressions to filter data easier to understand. It may be used to even make filtering procedures hard to be more straightforward. For example: ``(filtered_data = df.query('sales > @threshold')).

Another way to access data is by using the.loc[] and.iloc[] accessors. While `.iloc[]` is integer-based indexing, the `.loc[]` accessor is label-based. This flexibility opens many ways in which a developer can slice DataFrames. For instance, you can use the following code to choose particular rows and columns: ```subset = df.loc[5:10, ['column1', 'column2']. Pandas makes it easy to select individual columns, whereby one can construct a new DataFrame composed strictly of the appropriate columns by passing it a list of column names. To concentrate attention on particular aspects in a dataset for further scrutiny, this focused attention is very important. Aggregation is one of the basic methods for processing data, and it relies on summation functions such as sum, mean, count, etc. You can use Pandas to split a DataFrame into groups based on one or more keys and then apply aggregate methods to each group using the `groupby()` method.

Suppose you wish to find out the average salary per department and you have got a DataFrame containing your employee data. As thus, this could be done: The Python code for average salary is df.groupby('department')['salary'].mean(). This code returns a Series indexed by department, with an average wage for any group. When used with `groupby} }, the `agg} method lets you apply many aggregation functions in one go. For example, `summary = df.groupby('department').agg({'salary': ['mean', 'sum'], 'age': 'count'})`. In this case, it creates a summary DataFrame including the count of employees in each department, the average and total compensation, and so on.

There is also the function `pivot_table()` in Pandas used to make pivot tables with tabular data summaries. The usage of this will allow a user to select which columns to aggregate, the index and columns of the pivot table, as well as the algorithm to make those aggregations. It is most useful when an array needs to be aggregated in multiple dimensions. Here's an example : `` {python pivot = df.pivot_table(values='sales', index='month', columns='region', aggfunc='sum').}. This will generate a pivot table that succinctly gives an insight into data by summarizing total sales by month and region. A final important technique for much more complex data manipulation is reshaping data, which allows a programmer to reshape a DataFrame for particular analytical reasons. Pandas has several functions to reshape data: `melt()` and `pivot()`. A DataFrame that has a wide format may be melted into a long format, which is usually more appropriate for an analysis and display. Consider, for example, the following DataFrame. It contains data about sales of a number of products over several months:.

It is much easier now to see trends in each column by month with the transformed DataFrame because each row shows sales of one product for one given month. Instead, a long DataFrame simply pivots into a wide format using the `pivot()` trick. This is handy when generating summary tables. Say you have long format sales data in this DataFrame and you want to pivot this so that each product's sales is reported monthly: python pivoted = df.pivot(index='product', columns='month', values='sales') This operation returns a wide-format DataFrame, making it easier to compare various items because each column represents a month. Missing values are very prevalent in real-world datasets and may critically affect the processing of data. The integrity of an analysis depends upon the manner of handling such missing variables. Pandas contains several functions for finding and dealing with missing data.

Users can check if a DataFrame contains any missing values by using the `isnull()` method, which yields a boolean DataFrame indicating whether or not nulls are there. One example is Python's missing_data = df.isnull(). Pandas offers several ways to handle missing data: the `dropna()` function can be used for dropping rows or columns whose values are missing, and the `fillna()` method can be used to fill up missing values with particular values or derived statistics. Using Python

as an example, df.fillna(0, inplace=True) # Use 0 to fill up any missing data. The mean or median of the column can be used to fill in missing values. pythons mean_value = df['column_name'].mean()
df['column_name'].fillna(mean_value, inplace=True). These methods ensure that the analysis is not skewed or wrong conclusions are drawn due to missing data. Another powerful operation to manipulate data is merging datasets, by which data from multiple sources can be combined into one coherent DataFrame. The `merge()` function available in Pandas provides an effective means of performing database-style joins on DataFrames. As with the SQL joins, two DataFrames can be joined using the `merge()` function based on common columns. For instance, let's suppose two DataFrames: one containing personnel data and the other containing department data. The merge of these DataFrames based on a common key like {department_id} can be achieved like so:.

This will yield a new DataFrame containing only the rows where the DataFrames match each other. What kind of join is to be made, such as {inner{, {outer{, {left{, or {right{, depends on the `how} parameter. Pandas accommodates that datasets may be merged in several ways to accommodate joining on multiple keys aside from just one key. For example, in using pandas, the Python code would look like this: merged_df = pd.merge(df1, df2, on=['key1', 'key2'], how='outer'). This will merge the two DataFrames combining {key1} and {key2} and will include all records from both DataFrames. Once the data is prepared and combined, advanced transforms can now be applied to pull out new information or create new features. There are many ways of doing this with Pandas, including the use of the `apply()` method that enables users to apply custom functions to DataFrames, row-wise, or column-wise. There are many ways you can manipulate the flexible `apply()` method. For instance, you can create a user defined function and apply it to compute your transformation if you wanted to get the percentage of sales for each row compared to the total sales: The Python code for `def calculate_percentage(row)` is as follows: return row['sales'] / total_sales df['percentage'] = df.apply(calculate_percentage, axis=1). In this example, the rows of the DataFrame are passed to a user-defined function `calculate_percentage}`, which creates a new column with the calculated percentage. Another really great feature in Pandas is vectorized operations, which enable applying transformations directly to entire columns without an explicit loop. Here, you can use NumPy functions directly on the DataFrame as in the following example to apply a logarithmic transform on a column:. This operation applies the logarithmic adjustment in a vectorized way to the entire column, rather than looping over rows, which is not as efficient.

In summary, advanced Python data manipulation techniques can be precursors to efficient processing and analysis of data. Cleaning, transforming, and analyzing complex data through the use of libraries such as NumPy and Pandas can be productive for developers and data scientists while helping to squeeze out useful insights from the data. The Python toolkit offers the full capability to deal with data manipulation tasks, such as filtering or ordering data, data aggregation, and alteration. As demand for decisions based on data grows, professionals will be able to cope with increasingly complicated data challenges by mastering such sophisticated strategies. But tapping into and leveraging Python data handling capabilities allows one to thrive in data, perhaps working with large datasets, addressing missing values, or consolidating multiple data sources. Once these methods are implemented, analysts can improve efficiency, enhance the quality of their work, and ultimately make better judgments informed by data insights. Effective data manipulation and analysis will be a primal skill for the developers, analysts, and data scientist because the world is data pervasive and growing. Professionals, by accepting these sophisticated Python data manipulation methods, will lead in their domain and contribute to the ever-expanding corpus of knowledge and innovations within the field of data science.

CHAPTER IV

Object-Oriented Programming in Python

Classes and Objects

Python offers high-quality support for object-oriented programming that is a fundamental concept based on classes and objects. The paradigm places more emphasis on organizing software design around objects or data rather than on logic and functionalities. OOP makes the organization of code easier and more logical which lets the programmer write modular, scalable, and maintainable applications. Understanding classes and objects is an important prerequisite to maximizing your use of Python capabilities, as they provide the foundation for encapsulating information and features in a way that more accurately reflects real-world relationships and interactions.

A class is, by definition simply an outline for creating an object. It provides a data structure that has methods (functions) which manipulate the data and attributes or data. Such abstraction may then be exploited by classes to represent the complex systems by gathering actions and properties that are linked together. It enables the developers to maintain clear distinctions between the class's implementation and usage. For example, assume a class that one might wish to represent a `Car}. Features such as {color}, `make, and `model will probably be in the `Car} class, along with its methods of `drive(), `brake(), and `honk(). The encapsulation of attributes and behaviors makes it easier to manage the complexity of the code and understand the relationships between parts.

A class becomes instantiated whenever an object is created. An object can be described as a concrete realization of the class blueprint; it is an instance of a class. Since any object of a class is capable of carrying some or all of its own data, multiple objects of the same class can exist independently. Suppose you have a `Car} class; you may then create several `Car} objects with different attributes such as color and model year, for example, `myCar, `yourCar, and `neighborCar}. The benefit of OOP generation is that several instances can be gotten from a single class, which aids code reuse and makes one support a more structured framework. Encapsulation is one of the major advantages of using classes and objects. It is the bundling of data along with the methods working with it in one single unit, called the class. This preserves the integrity of data and also serves to manage the complexity involved. A developer can avoid unintentional changes to an object's internal state by controlling access to certain attributes or methods. This is commonly achieved in Python with the use of access modifiers such as private and protected. The protected attribute is readable and accessible both within the class and within subclasses, whereas a private attribute may only be accessed within the class. This facilitates a more stable code structure and allows for controlled interaction with the data.

Another significant concept in OOP that classes and objects facilitate is inheritance. A new class, sometimes referred to as a derived or child class can inherit properties and functions from an already existing class, referred to as a base or parent class through the inheritance mechanism. This, however, creates a class inheritance hierarchy and encourages code reuse. Consider for example a base class `Vehicle', then you can create derived classes such as `Car, Truck, Motorcycle", all having their unique behaviors and properties but inheriting common attributes and methods defined in `Vehicle'. It makes the code even more simple and easier to understand and modify it. Well, any derived classes will inherit changes made in the base class instantly if you ever need to change a common attribute or method. Another powerful feature in Python relevant to classes and objects is polymorphism. It allows different classes to be treated as if they are instances of the same class using a common interface. That means an operation can behave differently in multiple classes. For instance, you can call a method, say, `start()`, on any of the two class instances without having to be concerned with implementation details if the method is implemented in both the `Car` and `Truck` classes. Through polymorphism, developers write more generic and reusable code since it offers malleability as well as encourages code interoperability.

The composition strategy alternates inheritance. It refers to the process of constructing classes out of other classes. This generates a relationship such that the composed class can utilize the functionality of the component classes by having instances of other classes as attributes in the class. Unlike inheritance, this facilitates more flexibility because it is possible to create complex types by combining simpler, reusable components. A `Car` class could have an instance of a `Transmission` class and a `Car` class with an instance of a `Transmission` class could have an instance of a `Car` class. This design style encourages more modular design and can also result in a clearer separation of concerns. This is another very important aspect of objects and classes-the ability to declare class methods and static methods. The class methods can be invoked directly on the class itself without the need to first instantiate a class because class methods are attached to the class rather than the class instance. Usually, the factory methods which are able to generate class instances use them. However, static methods can be invoked by the classes and the instances and do not need any kind of access to either. Such utility functions that seem logically consistent and don't need the access to instance-specific data can be pretty useful in the usage of them.

The ideas of composition, inheritance, polymorphism, and encapsulation make the process of designing software stable. Classes and objects applied at the right places encourage code reuse and elaborate complex systems with simpler terms. Also, this modular approach makes it possible for the developers to work on separate classes without interfering in other's work, which makes it quite possible for people to collaborate on such big projects. Furthermore, the amount of flexibility that the class and objects provide ensures refactoring and maintenance get easier as the project progresses and the necessities do. Python provides a wide range of design patterns utilizing key concepts such as classes and objects to solve common problems in software design. Design patterns are standard ways of coding that address the most common design problems that the programmer faces; hence, they guide the programmer in writing more efficient and effective code. Most of the patterns, like Factory, Decorator, Observer, and Singleton, adopt OOP ideas in providing structured solutions. Learning these design patterns can be a tremendous boost to a developer's ability to build reliable software structures .

As developers work with classes and objects, testing is yet another consideration. Unit testing, testing individual components of the software so each works as expected, is significantly enabled by modularity in OOP. With the help of classes and objects, developers can create focused tests that check the behavior of certain code blocks without requiring the user to execute the entire program, thus isolating classes and their methods. This usually results in higher-quality software because developers can easily find and correct defects as soon as possible in the development process. Documentation is also very essential when using classes and objects in developing. Well-documented code is much easier for future developers-as well as original developers-to understand both what the code function does and the purpose of every class and method used in the code. This is particularly important with group work where a number of developers may be working on exactly the same code. Class documentation in Python has quite a few conventions and tools, such as docstrings, which let programmers write down their classes and methods' use and purpose right into the code.

The more complex software projects become, the better the coordination and effective communication of team members should be. It is there where inheritance, polymorphism, and encapsulation will come in handy, because they provide developers with a common vocabulary and well-defined framework. Their practical application can help teams produce software that is better understood, upgraded, and extended for better development. Classes and objects can impact performance in terms of resource usage. While object-oriented programming advocates for modularity and code reuse, there are cases where the cost to create and sustain objects becomes destructive to performance. Developers must strike a balance of all the advantages of OOP and demands for application performance. It could be needed in functional programming systems where performance is a critical factor to discern which parts would tend to benefit more from a more functional programming style.

As noted so far, the selected design patterns may also affect the performance of a program. Where some may optimize the use of resources, others are bound to increase costs. Programmers need to completely understand the trade-offs associated with each of these selections so that they make choices that contribute to project needs. Software development is changing fast, driven by the accelerated progression of technology. Two new paradigms in the programming languages are reactive and functional programming, which differ from one other in the type of structure they give to code. At the same time, original basic OOP concepts - classes and objects - can still be applied and are used mostly. Because so many of the modern programming languages combine aspects of functional programming with object-oriented programming, developers can use the suitable strategy for those use cases that fit best their needs.

Classes and objects form the fundamental building blocks of Python object-oriented programming that allow programmers to write and keep their code organized. Data encapsulation via classes with a strong focus on fostering code reuse and responsibility splitting can be very distinct. Polymorphism and inheritance help in interoperability and flexibility, allowing programmers to create complex systems in less time. Under all of the changes to the landscape of development of software, it still comes down to the understanding and proper use of classes and objects to write good code. The well-versed developers can create programs that not only perform well and meet a need but are also robust, scalable, and flexible enough to adapt when needs change. In the end, good use of classes and objects enables developers to construct software that will not be onerous for users to interact with and can later easily be developed upon and- if need be-maintained.

Inheritance and Polymorphism

It is what OOP, inheritance, and polymorphism are intended to produce in successful, scalable, and maintainable systems: the basic character of these ideas in the Python programming language carries over equally to the way most programmers approach system design and problem-solving. Knowing this about inheritance and polymorphism, developers will be in a much better position to write leaner code that is less likely to need to change much under changing requirements while improving the quality and dependability of software applications. Due to something called inheritance, classes can inherit properties and methods from a class already in existence. Such classes have sometimes been referred to as new classes, while the class whose properties and methods are inherited by a derived class is referred to as a base or parent class. This creates classes hierarchical such that code reuse is enhanced, and redundancy is eliminated. Here is a simple class hierarchy: the base class declared to be `Vehicle`, where common methods and properties, like `speed}, `fuel_type, and a method to start the engine apply to every car; then the particular classes would be `Car, Truck, or Motorcycle}. Thus, provided each of these classes defined with inheritance adds some special feature and methods, then they all inherit the {Vehicle} attributes and behaviors. Although the `Truck} class may include methods pertaining to cargo loading, the `Car} class might consist of characteristics for doors.

Among the most significant benefits of inheritance, code reuse is facilitated. Here, the common functionality can be specified only once in the base class so that they get inherited into the derived classes and the developers need not recreate that for every derived class. This finally results in less duplication of code as well as the codebase becomes efficient. For instance, suppose that within the `Vehicle` class, yet another method to calculate fuel economy is declared. All derived classes automatically inherit this capability; therefore, you do not have to change the same thing in every one of your subclasses. In other words, changes to the base class will automatically propagate to all the derived classes and inherently reduce the opportunities for inducing errors. Except for the avoidance of redundancy, inheritance also promotes extensibility. From the code in situ developers can easily create new derived classes whenever new functionalities or classes must be added to a system. For example, assuming a new class {Car} must be defined. The developer may now define a new class `ElectricCar that inherits all the methods and properties of `Car but adds specific features for an electric car. A new class in this case is defined, like:. Since extensibility makes the program more easily fitted to changing needs, along with the potential of giving a systematic way of class grouping related to each other, inheritance offers several positive effects.

Although inheritance presents many advantages, new issues that have to be resolved arise in the hands of the developers. The major problem comes up with the inheriting of multiple base classes by a derived class:. Though Python does support multiple inheritance, this can also cause problems-especially when this leads to something known as the "Diamond Problem." This arises in any case of a derived class which is inheriting from both of those base classes and two base classes have a common parent class. In some instances, Python has method resolution order that decides the method, sometimes bringing in some unexpected results. With the use of multiple inheritance, designers have to be very careful so that their designs will not get cluttered and remain understandable and manageable. One of the major features of inheritance is method overriding. Assuming that there is a method with some special names in a class which is declared in a derived class with the same name as a method in its base class. Then the method in the derived class overrides the method with the same name in the base class. Using such an approach, developers could override inherited methods in order to make them more suitable for a derived class. The `Car` class might override the `start()` method in the `Vehicle` class for including special start behavior appropriate to cars, while the `Truck` class might override it for higher engine specs. Therefore, it allows polymorphism and diversity to be increases by the ability of overriding inherited methods for a developer.

This ability of many classes to be considered instances of the same class via a common interface is known as polymorphism. It gives some extra code flexibility and dynamism, because one function may handle objects of many various types. Inheritance and polymorphism are very often used together in order to let methods in derived classes override and provide different implementations for a common behavior. There are two forms of polymorphism in Python: compile-time, or static, and runtime, or dynamic. This form of polymorphism describes the fact that one is allowed to declare many methods with the same name but with different parameters. The following best expresses function overloading: But Python does not allow the use of typical method overloading as, for example, in Java or C++. Nonetheless, the application of default and variable-length arguments does provide some dynamic behavior at runtime.

In Python, however, runtime polymorphism is used more often and realized through method overriding. This means that a method in a derived class can have its own implementation since it simply shares the same name as a method defined in the base class. It invokes on the actual class of the object, not on the type of the reference variable, the process called when a method is called on it. This makes the code more flexible and readable: a function can work on several types of objects. Suppose, for example, we create a function that is meant to be used on `Animal}\\\" objects. The method may invoke the `speak()\\\\\\\" method. This will invoke the `speak()` method declared in `Dog{ if you pass it an instance of the `Dog} class. If you pass an instance of the `Cat` class, then this will invoke the `Cat{ override `speak()` method. This is how polymorphism makes code clearer and more flexible for using a single function with many types of objects without problem.

Another widely applicable concept together with polymorphism is that of interfaces and abstract base classes, or ABCs. It can be used by a group of related courses such that they all can make use of the same interface without providing an implementation altogether. It supports abstract methods to be implemented by the derived class. This enables the derived classes to have flexibility in their implementation but, at the same time, it ensures some kind of contract to be followed. The abstract base classes enable extended programming since they portray polymorphism and make several classes that derive from a single class to be instances of an abstract class. Inheritance and polymorphism are widely practiced in real life, and the two make the designing of the program much more effective. These concepts enable encapsulation of a complex system with relationships that feel more intuitively natural than they do in code, so the code is more readable and understandable. For example, a GUI program can be represented using classes that are derived for buttons, sliders, and text fields, and a base class that represents a general UI component. Common shared attributes and methods created within the base class enable a part to provide its specific behavior.

Inheritance and polymorphism also allow the employment of design patterns: tried and tested solutions to recurrent problems that arise while programming, used by strategies like Strategy, Observer, and Factory, in order to introduce flexibility and order into the code. Strategy lets algorithms be described as classes, which makes it possible for developers to make the right decision at run time based on the situation. These rules make the software systems more maintainable. Inheritance and polymorphism can help create a better more orderly codebase. Polymorphism allows the programmer to take full advantage of general purpose code which will probably adapt to new requirements. Yet inheritance provides proper structure so the code, once properly explored and understood, is easier to vary. While inheritance and polymorphism have many advantages developers should be attentive to some disadvantages. One very common problem is the potential for the generation of extremely complex class hierarchies. " Inheritance may bring cleaner code but sometime creates complexity in hierarchies to manage and understand. It can be avoided if designers follow good design principles such as Single Responsibility Principle which says that a class should change for one and only reason. Designers should keep their designs to be understandable, hence keep the relationships between classes simple and obvious.".

Overuse of inheritance leads to establishing an overly connected system, where changes in one base class cause broad effects on all the derived classes and is difficult to add or change the system without some unforeseen consequences. This risk can be minimized further by coaching developers to favor composition over inheritance: a design philosophy that emphasizes building complex things from smaller, reusable components rather than depending only on class hierarchies. In this way, being composition-based, each part may be replaced or changed without affecting the system.

The second issue relates to the nature of Python: flexibility in data types, as well as the flexibility of changing variable assignments. That brings wonderful benefits but might also get some undesired behavior from the wrong source. To decrease the likelihood of implicit type conversion errors and even variable shadowing from being made, a developer must clearly and predictably code. Testing is yet another important area where override and polymorphism can come into the picture to ascertain the quality of the code. Do make sure that the derived classes fulfill the intent behavior defined in the base class while working with the context of polymorphic functions or classes. It is much more likely to catch behavioral differences and thus create in-depth tests crossing both the base as well as the derived classes in order to avoid regressions coming in through changes to the codebase. Support for inheritance and polymorphism remains high and flexible as the language evolves. Every new release of the language includes a lot of new features and improvements so that programmers receive even more tools to make an effective use of those concepts. Thus, with Python 3.5, type hints are presented through which programmers can describe their expectations about the types of data variables and return values for certain parameters. It is easier working with polymorphic functions, as the code becomes more comprehensible and allows for detection of errors at the development stage.

In addition to this, inheritance and polymorphism are impacted by the fact that Python is becoming an increasingly asynchronous language. Asynchronous synchronous functions, written in 'async def' syntax, have non-blocking execution; it allows programmers to write programs handling a large number of distinct kinds of activities simultaneously. This facility is very useful for applications like web servers and user interfaces, where they have to be interactive. Because the needs of the application are evolving towards the kinds of applications in contemporary user interface applications we do today with Python, then it requires knowing how asynchronous functions work and what their scope is, and hence now new avenues have opened up for the use of inheritance and polymorphism.

In a nutshell, the two most important concepts in object-oriented programming are inheritance and polymorphism. These enable developers to write flexible, scalable, and maintainable software. Although this is not to be confused with polymorphism per se, this is the power of reused and extensible code, which allows for good flexibility and adaptability of code. This implies that understanding two such new concepts helps the programmers make optimum utilization of Python's powers in developing programs which meet the needs of the current moment yet grow with time. Careful design, heeding these principles will enable developers to build a code quality and teamwork culture that is successful and long-lasting. Good programming techniques will also continue to focus on understanding and using inheritance and polymorphism in an increasingly complex technological world. The ability to use abstract base classes to realistically simulate class hierarchy relationships and to design patterns shall eventually characterize how truly great and effective systems in software are constructed. These ideas will be much more precious as the discipline of software development matures. As heritage and polymorphism offer many advantages, but simplicity and maintainability are virtues, wise developers should make proper decisions. Developers can thoroughly exploit inheritance and polymorphism for high-quality software in which user needs are met and changing requirements change easily, when there is a rigorous and pragmatic approach to design.

Encapsulation, Abstraction, and Decorators

Encapsulation, abstraction, and decorators are some of the three fundamental concepts of object-oriented programming (OOP), which enhance code organization, flexibility, and maintainability. Based on these concepts, Python is among the most widely used languages today. For developers to write good, neatly arranged programs that deal with complexity and hide data efficiently, they must have a good grasp of abstraction and encapsulation. However, decorators provide a special way to modify functions or methods' behavior and offer code reuse, which all leads to increased functionality without having to alter the original source. All these concepts together provide a good solid foundation for building effective, scalable, and maintainable software.

The encapsulation concept refers to bundling data with operations carried out on it in one entity - often a class. This theory is originated from the fact that the internal state of an object can be hidden from the outside world by restraining direct access to some of the components of the object. By encapsulating the data, developers can enhance data integrity and security because it prohibits unauthorized access and modification. Public, protected, and private access modifiers are used very frequently in Python for achieving encapsulation. Subclasses can access the protected members, which are intended to be used within the class itself and are not designed to be accessed externally; public attributes and methods are accessible from the exterior of the class. The private members with a double underscore prefix basically hide the sensitive information and implementation details from view, and they are not allowed to enter the class.

Encapsulation mainly promotes segregation of duty within a software program. Code partitioned into separate classes, where each class is responsible for a set of functionalities can be easily developed by programmers in modular and reusable building blocks. The code also becomes easier to read, test, and maintain due to modularity. For instance, suppose you have a banking application in which the `Customer` class holds the information of the customer. This class may also include operations on customers' accounts, such as deposit and withdrawal. In this way, the linking of the operations that handle customer's data altogether will make the code more readable and self-explanatory. This ability also allows for better control over whom to allow access to and who is allowed to update a certain data. The developer can enforce the valid constraints or rules for modifications to occur on an object's state by including getter and setter methods. For example, a {BankAccount` class could include a deposit method that, before modifying the account balance, insures the deposit amount is valid. This provides stronger code and protects it against more probable errors, while also protecting the data integrity. It is easier to control application component interactions if an object's internal state is modified through well-defined interfaces.

Another significant benefit of encapsulation is the possibility of changing the inner functionality of a class without impacting the external code that relies on its functionality. Since users work with an object based on the provided public interface, developers are free to modify the inner operation of the class-for example, change method implementation or make changes to data storage-without affecting any existing functionality. This is particularly helpful for larger applications where many objects might depend on others. That way, developers can update their code over time without breaking backward compatibility due to encapsulated data and behavior.

Abstraction is the technique of making complex systems understandable by modeling classes around inherent characteristics and operations of real-life things. Abstraction is closely related to encapsulation. Abstracting aims at reducing complexity by excluding useless information and making available only the appropriate parts to the external world. ABCs and interfaces in Python are often used in creating abstraction. An abstract base class defines abstract methods, which need to be implemented by all derived classes to present a common interface to a group of related classes. This creates a contract that lets derived classes offer their implementation but ensures they work based on some structure.

The key strength of abstraction is that it takes away the implementation details from the hands of developers and allows them to focus on higher-level functionality. For instance, in a graphics design application, `Circle}`, `Rectangle`, and `Triangle} would be particular derivative classes making concrete implementations of common methods like `draw()` and `resize()`, while an abstract base class called `Shape} defines the generalizations of these methods. Developers can then work uniformly with forms without care for which specific kinds of shapes. Code can be developed more generally, and thus more reusable, if writers communicate with the abstract interface instead of communicating directly with the specific implementations. Abstraction also makes code easier to read and maintain. Developers can make the code they are producing more readable by declaring a class's interface explicitly. Other developers get to understand all about the purpose and functionality of a class when it has a clear set of methods and properties. This is particularly important in team environments where multiple developers are working on the same code base. Well-defined abstraction rules also improve interaction and recognition by the team members, which decreases the potential for misunderstanding and mistakes.

Second, abstraction allows the development of software architecture and design patterns. Abstract classes and interfaces are preconditions for many design patterns, such as Factory, Observer, and Strategy patterns, because they provide loose coupling between components. Shared interfaces make independence possible among components of an application. The reason is, extensions and changes are possible very easily for software systems, and features and enhancements can be added without much need for rewriting. The special feature of Python, called decorators, can increase the functionality of functions or methods to perform more work without changing any original code. A decorator is, in fact a function that takes an argument from another function, augments its behavior, and returns a new function with new properties. Decorators are often used to add pre- or post-processing actions to operations performed, such as performance monitoring, permission checks, or logging. It is possible to use this method to apply decorators to many functions without making their implementations overly complex, which promotes reuse of the code and separation of concerns.

The two concepts of abstraction and encapsulation are very close to decorators because decorators encapsulate the routine actions into reusable components so that the developers can help focus the basic logic of their functions on the actual duties of the functions. Another way of getting useful insight into performance without having to change individual functions is to design a logging decorator that, whenever it is applied to any function it wraps, automatically logs the execution time of the function. This allows programmers to add the kinds of overarching concerns-to error handling and logging, for instance-without losing sight of the functionality of their core programs.

Checking input parameters or implementing access control can also be done using decorators. For instance, the decorator can be used on a function so that only authorized users will execute it. The main function can be separated from the log-in mechanism, in an effort to help developers build a code base less hard to maintain and purer. This separation of concerns is one of the distinguishing features of good software design, and thus this makes it possible to deal with different parts of an application separately. Beautifully, decorators do not only make code more readable and maintainable but are also consistent with the DRY philosophy. People will not repeat code in several functions; instead, shared functionality can be captured in a decorator and used throughout where required. This way, the amount of duplicate code is reduced and the codebase remains consistent. For instance, to guarantee uniformity and centralization of the validation logic, it might be developed as a single validation decorator and then applied on all functions needing input validation.

Among the available Python decorators, `@staticmethod`, `@classmethod`, and `@property` enrich the class methods. The use of the decorator `@staticmethod` enables one to call a method without necessarily having to make an instance. The decorator `@classmethod` allows one to call a method from the class itself instead of calling it over instances of the class. The use of the decorator `@property` helps the developers intuitively access attributes with less effort, by enabling them to design getter and setter methods. Such build-in decorators call for attention to how powerful and flexible decorators are in Python and how they support improvement of functionality without adding complexity to the codebase. Though the decorators can be used only with built-in functions, developers are able also to make custom decorators for particular work. Using this, the behavior of functions inside an application is possible to change highly flexibly. Examples of such kind include extending custom decorators to log function calls, handle exceptions, enforce type checks, etc. For instance, once these decorators are declared, developers can use them everywhere in the code base of an application consistently, which automatically decreases the chances of errors and makes maintenance much more manageable.

In addition to encapsulation and abstraction, one needs to consider how these concepts interlink and increase one another's strength in the broader aspect of software architecture. Together, abstraction and encapsulation enable building modular and reusable components. Encapsulation can enable developers to bunch methods along with associated data. The rather complex system with a lot of features could become relatively simple by exposing only those features that are actually needed. Synergism leads to a comprehensible, easier-to-maintain, and easier-to-exploit codebase. The principles of abstraction and encapsulation give decorators the strength since they permit developers to insert or alter functionality in a clean, modular manner. Developers can append further behaviors onto encapsulated methods or functions without modifying the underlying logic using decorators. The segregation of responsibilities helps to make the code more readable and maintainable; developers can focus on the most important features while using decorators to address the conflicts between intersecting problems.

Encapsulation, abstraction, and decorators have many real-world applications into the works of web development, analysis of data, artificial intelligence, and others. These ideas applied the inner workings of web programming, for instance, using frameworks like Flask and Django to offer an organized method of building online applications. Thanks to encapsulation, developers can define views, controllers, and models as separate components while abstraction helps communicate with these components by defining clearly defined interfaces. Web frameworks commonly have requests handling with decorators and middleware, authentication, etc, so complicated actions can be implemented modularly. Both the encapsulation and abstraction concepts play a significant role in data analysis since they help one organize code for data manipulation and visualization. These concepts are applied by libraries, such as Pandas, in the development of high-level abstractions when working with tabular data. The use of data structures like DataFrames through Pandas encapsulates data structures and promotes readability and ease of use; further, users are allowed to handle sophisticated data sets using common methods. Data analysts and scientists can make their workflows more effective and apply caching or any other performance-monitoring tool by applying decorators in data analysis.

These ideas are implemented through libraries such as TensorFlow and PyTorch, which facilitate flexible and composable frameworks for building machine learning models. While abstraction simplifies the design of complex neural networks, encapsulation allows developers to specify models as unique objects, with their own properties and behaviors. Abstraction, encapsulation, and decorators are also critical concepts in the machine learning and artificial intelligence domain. The decorators allow researchers to monitor the success of their models without interfering with the main logic by applying them on training methods that add some custom logging or metrics tracking.

In a nutshell, the key ideas of encapsulation, abstraction, and decorators enable programmers to design structured, adaptable, and maintainable software systems. By the binding of data and methods together, encapsulation promotes data protection and modularity while abstraction reduces complexity by exposing only those parts of an object that are pertinent. Decorators add functionality without altering the underlying code, providing developers with a clean, reusable way to introduce cross-cutting concerns. They coalesce to form the basis of good software design, where developers make reliable systems that can evolve in response to changing needs over time. The Python programmer will develop quality software that meets the needs of users and that stands the test of time because they master encapsulation, abstraction, and decorators.

CHAPTER V

Managing Files and External Libraries

File Input and Output

Programming programs allow file input/output in order to manipulate data stored in files. File input/output in Python is very simple yet powerful functionality, which allows programmers to read from and write in files, this properly handling large volumes of data. This section ranges from simple text-file-processing scripts to complex systems for managing database and web application data storage. Any Python developer who wants to use a large percentage of the language's possible functions and who needs to persist data between invocations of a program must know how to do file I/O.

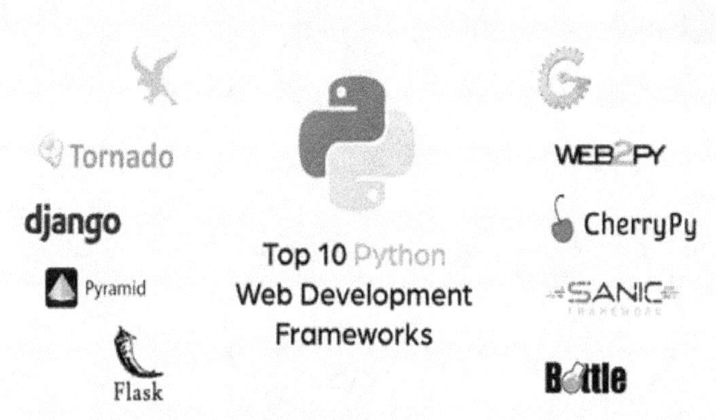

Files are treated as streams of data in Python, and the language provides a large number of built-in functions and techniques that serve to manage files. The most basic file I/O operations involve opening, reading, writing, and closing a file. There exist numerous methods provided by the standard library of Python to perform each of these actions. It is important to understand these techniques and how they work in order to manage files effectively. The first tool used when dealing with files is the `open()` function, which takes the file name and the mode of operation as its two main arguments. The mode determines what you will use the file for - reading, writing, or appending. Commonly used modes for opening a file in Python are 'r' for reading, 'w' for writing, 'a' for appending, and 'r+' for reading and writing. A program only reads the contents of a file when it opens it in read mode. If the file does not exist, an error is shown. Conversely, if you open a file in write mode, all the information in it will be erased and, if you do not already have one, one will be created. The append mode of new data can be written without affecting existing content by appending it to a file. To avoid losing data and access the file properly, one should understand these modes.

Once a file has been opened, carry out the needed operations on a file by reading from or writing to it. Besides all those ways to read material from a file, Python provides `read()`, `readline()`, and `readlines()`. The `read()` method is handy when the file is small enough to fit into memory as a whole, because it reads the contents of the file from top to bottom and returns it as a single string. On the other hand, the `readline()` function reads in lines one at a time that makes it useful for controlling the reading, especially when dealing with large files. In case it is given the option to read over every line in a file, the `readlines()` function will return a list of strings, each of which represents one line in the file. A combination of the size of the file being read and the specific requirements of the application determine the best reading method.

Writing to files in Python is quite easy too. A list of strings can be written to a file with the `writelines()}` function, where as a string can be written with the `write()`

method. But note that the file needs to be opened in either write or append mode before you can write to it. Data will be overwritten in a file that has already been opened in write mode. Before writing to the file, developers must choose the appropriate mode to ensure data safety. Another newline characters are often encountered while writing to a file especially to format the output correctly when writing multiple lines. Closing a file is an important step in the file I/O operation. After all the necessary reads or writes are performed on a file, it should be closed by calling its 'close()' method. Closing a file frees up all the associated system resources and also persists any changes that were performed on it. Failure to close a file can result in many unexpected behaviors, memory leaks, and more importantly damage your data. The `with` statement is an automatic file-closure mechanism in Python that really makes file handling simple and minimalistic that reduces the scope for error. Indeed, if there is a mistake, the file opened with a `with` statement is closed at the moment when the block of code within the statement goes out of scope.

Understanding file paths, which describe the location of a file in the filesystem, is the other part of dealing with files. A file path in Python can be absolute or relative. The former gives the complete address of a file starting with the root directory, while the latter displays the location of the file relatively from the current working directory. Correct file opening requires the right file path; Python provides the following functions, `os.path.join()}` and `os.path.abspath()}` among others, to manipulate paths:. Developers should be very careful with file paths, especially in changing environments or implementing apps. Another crucial characteristic of Python file I/O is error handling. In any number of reasons from a missing file, to not having permission to read the file, to running into I/O problems, files will not always be readable. This requires proper exception handling strategies, which entails a `try` and `except` block. Exceptions that could easily happen in file I/O operations can be caught by the developers by putting file operations within a `try` block and then taking suitable action: reporting an error, giving some form of user feedback, or falling back to whatever else you want to happen. The ability to handle errors makes an application stronger and prevents it from happening with an unplanned crash.

Another more popularly used application of Python is the I/O function file in text processing forms. They are just simple plain text files that can store data within its normal text format. Heavy-duty text-manipulation and -processing tools are offered by Python in dealing with text files. This can range from several ways of using string methods on search patterns, filtering data based on specified standards, and presenting data into other formats. The use of regular expressions in the processing of text files often comes in handy when searching and replacing complex patterns, which helps extract valuable data from big datasets. Python is pretty lenient with regard to its string manipulation capabilities, meaning many developers are able to code fairly quickly using text files in various ways. In addition to text files, Python supports binary file operations. Binary files are more compressed and efficient to store such massive quantities of data because they store data in an unreadable format to humans. Some examples of the binary file are picture files, music files, and proprietary data formats. When you're working with a binary file, a file should be opened in 'b' mode, indicating that the file is made up of binary data. Although data is considered bytes not as strings while reading and writing binary files, procedures are almost the same as those for reading and writing text files. Making this distinction is important for proper data processing since mishandling binary data may lead to data damages or loss.

Yet another format that Python supports text file. Libraries like `csv`, `json`, and `pickle` provides further functionality when reading from and writing to formats. In cases of comma-separated values, it is quite handy to include the `csv` module during writing as it simplifies the work of tiding tabular data. These libraries enable the developer in effective management of operation regarding import and export related to the data which itself facilitates interaction with the external systems and data sharing between many applications. The JSON format has gained popularity for data interchange because it is easy to read and understand. Developers can quickly serialize a Python object into JSON and deserialize JSON data back into Python objects using `json`, the built-in module of Python. This allows communication between many systems quite smoothly, and it is useful for web apps that wish to exchange data with servers or APIs. Developers can make their applications much more interactive and responsive if they learn how to work with JSON files.

The `pickle` module in Python can serialize and deserialize objects in Python, or in other words, "pickle" whole Python objects from a file if the data structure is too complex to be serialized. Its functionality is significantly useful for applications with persistent storage of the complicated data types, such as custom classes or data structures. Using this module ensures that programmers preserve their data between executions of the program and makes application operation and data management better. All applications for logging and monitoring rely on file input/output. Developers can observe performance, trace the actual execution of a program, and even debug runtime problems by writing logs to a file. Python's `logging` module provides a stable logging architecture that enables developers to establish multiple log levels, formats, and outputs. An important insight into the behavior of their program can be gained by developers through the monitoring of significant events and errors written to a file. This makes it easier to identify problems and optimize performance.

Data backup and recovery is another important functionality of file I/O. Frequent file backups ensure that essential data is protected when system crashes or data loss occur. Developers can prevent accidental overwrites or corruption by implementing automated backup routines for copying files securely on a recurring basis. File I/O functions play the most important role in data handling and recovery. They also help protect data from possible losses and ensure continuous business. File I/O is critical to big data processing in scientific computing and data processing. Python can easily read and write data files thanks to its ability to work hand-in-hand with data analysis libraries such as NumPy and Pandas. For example, pandas offers data manipulation consistent APIs and easy ways of reading data from SQL, Excel and CSV databases. Thus, with file I/O capabilities pre-processing data, doing analysis and storing results flows so much better in the hands of data scientists to improve significantly.

Cloud computing and remote data storage solutions are part of the scope for file I/O. Knowing how to work with files in cloud environments becomes more important with the speedy growth rate of using cloud services to process and store data. Libraries like `boto3 give developers the power to directly read and write files from the cloud, thus offering an interface with cloud storage systems such as Amazon S3. These dynamics allow applications to be built dynamically without taking advantage of the significant flexibility and availability of cloud resources. Thus, security has to always be an issue when dealing with file I/O, especially if dealing with private or sensitive data. Secure access to files must be implemented along with encryption in order to maintain data integrity and prevent unauthorized access. Modules in Python like {cryptography} have the highest possible capabilities for encrypting files and protecting data at storage and transmission. This is how developers can protect user's data as well as meet regulatory standards while performing file I/O operations.

To put it briefly, file input and output represent a fundamental feature of Python programming that enables programmers to read from and write to files fairly easily. Effective data manipulation involves mastering different types of file I/O operations which include opening, reading writing, and closing files. The number of built-in file handling functions and modules, in addition to the support of many file formats, and with error handling, allow developers to create reliable apps that are easy to handle data. File input/output (I/O) is always critical; that is because it forms an important constituent part of data administration, analysis, and application development in a wide variety of fields even as technology advances. Mastering file I/O in Python is directly beneficial to developers to attain a more effective personality as programmers or coders and prepare high-quality robust data-handling programs.

Working with CSV, JSON, and XML Data

Data management, in this day and age, would be the most crucial part of programming because most, if not all, produce or consume heaps of data every day. Among the most utilized data formats for storage and transfer include CSV (Comma-Separated Values), JSON (JavaScript Object Notation), and XML (eXtensible Markup Language). Each one has different characteristics and purposes-from a developer's point of view as well as from the viewpoint of a data analyst. Arguably, one of the most used programming languages in web development, automation, and data research is Python. The efficient arrangement and processing of data using the different types of data in Python depend on the ability to handle multiple data types.

The simplest and most fundamental way data can be stored is through CSV. They are plain text data represented as rows and columns. Every row is a record while each column is a field. "Comma-Separated Values" gets its name from the fact that it uses commas as delimiters for values in each line. Being straightforward and very easy to use, CSV files are particularly useful for tabular data, which can be found in databases and spreadsheets. Such data files can easily be developed using text editors and spreadsheet applications, such as Microsoft Excel or Google Sheets, and they happen to be human-readable. These features make CSV files extremely popular for the exchange of data among various numbers of systems and applications. Compact size and simplicity of parsing are some of the major advantages of CSV files. CSV files have an ability to upload and process the data quickly because they do not depend on heavy parsing logic like that of some more complex format. Thus, CSV files would be fairly optimal for big datasets, especially in scientific computing and data analysis applications. But despite all these advantages, there is still a limitation with CSV files:. All values will be kept as strings because these do not have a standard way of showing whether data type is present. This might become confusing, especially when handling dates and numbers. Using CSV files is not very ideal when trying to capture complicated relationships between data, because CSV does not support nested or hierarchical data types.

Python developers would often make use of the built-in module `csv}` in dealing with CSV files. It has a number of methods and classes to read from and write to CSV files. A CSV file may be read with `csv.reader`, returning a list of values for every row. This simplifies data manipulation and analysis, as developers can easily traverse rows and access required fields quickly. By using a `csv.writer`, it's possible to store data in a structured way as a CSV file by creating and writing a file. The `csv` module is one of the de-facto Python modules for managing tabular data, primarily due to the ease.

Other than CSV, there's JSON, which is the lightest format of exchanging data. JSON is a nice choice for web applications as well as web APIs since it's nice to read and write for humans, and also pretty easy for machines to parse and build. The format is capable to represent complex data structures; it supports arrays and nested objects, based on a very foundation - the key-value pair. This is because JSON is an extremely flexible utility when it comes to exchanging data among several systems, particularly in terms of online services and the need for structured data to be requested and distributed as well. JSON's compatibility with other programming languages such as Python, JavaScript, and Ruby makes it, perhaps the biggest strength. An all-purpose solution for data exchange is possible simply because JSON can be easily implemented using any programming language by developers. In addition, because JSON is a less verbose format, it transmits data faster and saves a file of smaller size compared to XML, which makes the efficiency particularly helpful when working with massive datasets or in situations that are performance-critical, such as real-time applications or data streaming.

Python's built-in `json` module allows you to work with JSON data that has built-in methods for both encoding and decoding the JSON data. The method `json.loads` parses JSON data from a string and `json.load}` can be used when reading JSON data from a file. On the other hand, the json.dump and json.dumps methods write JSON data directly to a file or Python objects to JSON strings, respectively. This makes it easier for developers to work with JSON data due to `json` module's flexibility and ease, which allow fast serialization and deserialization of complicated data structures.

Although CSV and JSON are great data exchange formats, many people still want to represent their hierarchical data in XML. Because XML is technically a markup language that allows developers to create their own tags, it is also well-suited for representation of all sorts of data structures. Applications requiring rich data representations, such as configuration files, document repositories, and data interchange between different systems, are particularly well-suited for it. XML files are so rich in the format because they can contain mixed content, nested elements, and attributes. The major benefit of XML is its extensibility. More flexibility in the representation of data is mainly because developers can specify their own tags and structure. Furthermore, XML supports definitions of schema using technologies such as Document Type Definition (DTD) and XML Schema Definition (XSD) that facilitate validating the format and content of an XML document. Thus, with this validation feature, data integrity can be facilitated during data transfer from one system to another whose needs are not the same.

However, there are disadvantages with XML as well. A major problem is verbosity: XML files are typically larger than CSV or JSON files, because with any element, you have both an opening tag and a closing tag. Suppose that opening tags in XML, not counting attributes, have length 15, closing tags have length 6. This could give much longer parsing times, as well as more storage needs, for large datasets. Furthermore, despite the fact that XML is a human-readable format, interacting with it may be more complex compared to simpler formats like CSV and JSON. A usual Python programmer will deal with XML data via such libraries as `xml.etree.ElementTree}` and `lxml}`. The `ElementTree` module provides convenience and simplification for parsing and generating

XML documents. The trees can be browsed; XML data from files or texts can be loaded into the application, and elements can be fetched or changed based on demands. Performance is much better, and more capable with the `lxml` library, especially for complex XML documents. In fact, developers can put together applications that require hierarchical data representations using these tools.

Python has lots of modules and utilities that make the transition smooth while converting data into different formats. Developers can, therefore, pick the most appropriate format for their specific needs by just converting the data from CSV to JSON or XML and vice versa. Flexibility is quite helpful where, by default, stakeholders on either side may insist on different formats or where data needs to be shared across several systems. Application developers can develop effective interoperability across several applications by optimizing the data-conversion procedures by third-party tools and Python standard libraries. Data analysis is one more area that uses CSV, JSON, and XML data. Before this data is used for analysis in data science and machine learning, the developer has to import and preprocess it in one of the formats above. Libraries such as Pandas provide native functionalities for working with CSV and JSON data easily.

Such libraries allow for easy loading, manipulation, and visualization of data, where using Pandas, developers may read CSV files into data frames, clean and transform the corresponding data, and export the resulting data in their chosen formats. The functionalities supporting CSV and JSON while keeping Pandas makes the process of data analysis much straightforward, and the conclusions drawn by the data scientists spend less time on minute details regarding the management of data. There is no support for directly reading from XML files using Pandas, but developers can make use of libraries such as {xml.etree.ElementTree} along with Pandas to convert the XML data to a format appropriate for analytical purposes. Development on the same types of analysis possible with CSV or JSON can be achieved using extracted information from XML documents and making it a DataFrame. The ability to work with several formats is very important in data-driven contexts because the difference between the ability to work with several formats and being limited to one format makes a big difference between the quality of analysis and decision-making.

Working with CSV, JSON, and XML data often becomes important in building dynamic web applications. JSON is so frequently used in the transmission of data among other services by web APIs because it is lightweight and easy to use. The use of AJAX requests in conveying JSON data to the client-side while developing web applications allows the developer to update the information without refreshing the entire page-an important factor of smooth interaction. XML is also used by most web services especially with Web applications, which often require complex data structures. Also, there are other technologies like SOAP, Simple Object Access Protocol, in which software application communicates with the other application on the Internet. In these, XML has played an important role. The second thing is that CSV files can be given as downloadable datasets, whereby customers can obtain data in some form which can easily inputted in spreadsheet packages or any application. To make communication with external systems and exchange valid and structured data, many developers use XML-based APIs. Web service integrators must know how to deal with XML data since it allows them to provide stable solutions that will interact with other systems.

Another area where handling of CSV, JSON, and XML data can bring out highly valuable information is in data visualization. During integration of data into visualization frameworks like Matplotlib or Seaborn, developers may develop illuminating graphs and charts that make for effective and accurate transfer of information. In fact, data visualization is an outstanding technique through which patterns can be identified and trends understood and passed on to stakeholders as findings. Having to work with diverse formats of data, developers can collect a large number of datasets and present them in excellent forms contributing effectively to the overall effect their study will make. Besides, error correction and data validation are very significant skills when dealing with CSV, JSON, and XML data. Data verification regarding accuracy and integrity becomes necessary when working with an external data source. Applications like financial systems and medical applications, where data accuracy is of prime importance, will have to seek special attention in this aspect. Developers should provide complete validation tests to ensure that the developed data is valid by following the expected format and constraints in preventing errors and data corruption.

Error handling is particularly important when dealing with data formats: while there are many ways things can go wrong while loading and processing, developers are certainly going to encounter corrupted XML structures, malformed JSON, or simply bad CSV. Developers can address these problems elegantly by having good error-handling procedures in place - for reporting failures and to provide the user with useful feedback.

Introduction to External Libraries

Developers and data analysts have to be skilled and able to handle different forms of data formats. Between these formats, the most common ones used are CSV, JSON, and XML. Based on their characteristics and uses, there can be different forms of data transmission and representation. Currently, programming demands an awareness of these data types, primarily in the types of languages used nowadays, such as Python, which are easy and flexible to use.

Of the most common data formats for the usual data transformation activities, one of the easiest to use is the CSV file. They are a set of text files with tabular data that is structured into rows representing single records and columns representing fields or attributes. A comma separates each item in a row, thus making it easy to process and parse. The CSV format has emerged as extremely popular due to its simplicity, particularly for those datasets that are naturally represented in a table-the sort as those of relational databases and spreadsheets. CSV files are easily developed and human-readable and can be edited using simple text editors or spreadsheet applications. The main advantage of CSV files is that they are compact. They are extensively used in data interchange because they can be generated and read by a wide range of systems and programming languages. One great advantage of CSV files is that they tend to be much smaller in file size than other, more verbose formats such as XML, and not having to accommodate complicated syntax or structure lets them load and process faster when working with large data sets. Creation and edition are also very easy, so perfect for cases where rapid data imports and exports are necessary in applications of all kinds. CSV files are very simple, though, and this brings out a few drawbacks. To start with, all values are treated as strings since they are ready only to accept plain text and no other forms of data type. It confuses dealing with dates or numbers. Instead, CSV files will not be the best for complex datasets because there is no uniform way to represent nested data structures or hierarchy.

The developers of the program make use of the inbuilt `csv` module of Python for processing the CSV data. This will easily allow reading from and writing to the CSV file. Developers can read through a CSV file using the `csv.reader`, which returns a list of values to every row. This feature simplifies simple data manipulation since developers can easily get access to some fields and loop over rows without requiring complex parsing algorithms. Similarly, using the csv.writer method developers can easily create and write to CSV files. Due to the efficient and straightforward architecture of the csv module, it is one of the top choices of Python developers working with tabular data.

JSON is a lightweight data-interchange format that has taken widespread popularity, especially on the simplicity of the CSV format, for web applications. In addition, since it's meant to be easily readable by both computers and people, data generation and processing may be performed pretty fast. The format can represent complex data structures such as arrays and nested objects and is based upon a set of key-value pairs. JSON is probably the best choice for sending data across different systems, especially in web services and APIs. It has provided the kind of flexibility that is required in the transaction of structured data. One of its greatest strengths is that JSON is available for use with many computer languages. JSON is a versatile option for exchanging data since it can easily be mapped into programs such as Python, JavaScript, and Ruby. Because the format uses relatively simple syntax, files are much smaller than they are in XML, making it more efficient and speedier when transferring data. It is ideal for applications of humongous datasets or real-time data transfer.

The Python built-in `json` module enables developers to manipulate JSON data directly. It offers convenient methods for encoding and decoding JSON data. Instead of the `json.dumps` method, the `json.load` method is used to read JSON data from a file; instead of `json.loads`, the method `json.loads` is used to parse JSON data from a string. On the other hand, developers can write JSON data to a file or convert Python objects to

JSON strings with the `json.dump` and `json.dumps` methods, respectively. With the simple functionality of the `json` module, developers can easily work with JSON data because it is really fast to serialize and deserialize complex data structures.

Although CSV and JSON find large usage in many applications, it is the one format whereby XML is most commonly used for display purposes when the data is hierarchical in nature. Since XML happens to be a markup language that will enable programmers to create their own tags, it may very well express an extremely large class of data structures very flexibly. Applications that involve complex data representations, such as configuration files, documents and transfer of data from one system to another, are particularly well suited for XML. As compared to CSV and JSON, XML files provide deep structure for the organization and representation of data because their supporting components, attributes, as well as mixed content may be nested.

Extensibility is one of the primary benefits of XML. This is because the developers can express any tags they want and structure. Additionally, XML also supports schema definition through DTD and XSD technologies, whereby programmers can also check the format and content of an XML document. This validation aspect can be used to ensure integrity, especially when switching between systems with differing needs. XML also has its downsides, though. One major problem is verbosity: since the opening and closing tags for every element must appear in XML files, XML files tend to become very long compared to equivalent CVS or JSON files. For example, verbosity can result in more challenging storage space and processing times when dealing with big data. In addition, even though XML is human-readable, its complexity may make it more difficult to work with than simpler alternatives like CSV and JSON. Practitioners of Python typically rely on libraries like `xml.etree.ElementTree} and `lxml} to work with XML. The module `ElementTree` indeed makes the job of parsing and creating an XML document simplified and efficient. The developers can browse through a tree structure, load XML data from files or texts, and extract or change elements appropriately. The `lxml` library enables more sophisticated capabilities as well as better performance with its help, which is particularly useful with complicated XML documents. Using these tools, developers can therefore write applications which have a hierarchical data representation or manipulate XML data.

Over time, technology often breeds a new desire for data conversion from one format to another. Data usually comes in some format at the time it is accumulated and saved but has to be converted to be useful to another application or system. For example, let us suppose that we have a dataset formatted as a CSV for analysis by spreadsheet software. However, the dataset must be converted to JSON so that it can become part of the web application. In this regard, Python has libraries and tools that provide developers with an opportunity to choose the best representation according to their needs, as they make easy data conversion between these formats. Data is usually read in one format, transformed as necessary, and then written out into another format as part of a conversion. To convert from CSV to JSON, for instance, you would need to read the CSV file, extract the right information, and then formulate it into key-value pairs before saving it out as a JSON file. Just like the conversion of JSON to XML, converting JSON to XML involves data processing of JSON, establishing the required structure in XML, then writing a file. All these are processes during the process. This is useful where different stakeholders require data in different forms or if data needs to be shared between different systems.

Data analysis is also another area that will require the use of CSV, JSON, and XML data. In order to be analyzed in domains such as data science and machine learning, developers have to import and preprocess the data in one of these two formats. Good functionalities for working with CSV and JSON data are provided by libraries like Pandas, and it makes data loading, manipulation, and visualization quite simple. Developers use pandas to import CSV files into DataFrames, clean and transform data, and export data in formats varied enough. Combining the powers of CSV and JSON together with pandas makes it easier for data scientists to conduct more analysis on data, where sometimes spending less time on details regarding data management can be tamed by more time concluding. Although Pandas does not natively read the XML file, developers can rely on libraries like {xml.etree.ElementTree} together with Pandas to parse the data from XML into a form that will be suitable for analysis. You can utilize XML information in such a manner that developers could perform the same kind of analysis that they can do on CSV or JSON information by extracting relevant information from the XML documents and then turning it into a DataFrame. This flexibility is of prime importance in data-driven contexts since the ability to work with different formats of data will dramatically enhance the quality of analysis and decision-making.

When it comes to developing web applications, interaction with CSV, JSON, and XML data becomes even more important. Due to its simplicity and lightweightness, JSON is largely used for the purpose of data exchange in web APIs. During the development of web applications, developers can use AJAX requests to send JSON data to the client side and, hence, make easy the refreshing and communication without reloading the whole page. This aspect improves the users' experience because content is dynamic and, therefore updates on input from users almost immediately. CSV files can also extensively be availed with web development. They are often used to provide datasets that can be downloaded, giving users access to data in a format that makes it easy to input into spreadsheet programs or other applications. Because it enables the local manipulation and exploration of the data, this is quite helpful for applications involving data analysis. Useful to developers, data may be represented in CSV format for consumers to explore and interpret it appropriately for their needs.

In addition to JSON and CSV, XML remains an important standard for representing hierarchical data structures associated with web services. It plays a key part in specific technologies that represent a way to enable communication with online services, namely, SOAP (Simple Object Access Protocol). Developers tend to use XML-based APIs for seamless interaction with external systems and data exchange in a validated and structured form. For developers undertaking web service integration, it is pretty much important for them to understand how to deal with XML data as this will enable them to develop reliable solutions that can interface with other systems. Dealing with data in the formats of CSV, JSON, and XML provides very insightful information in the area of data visualization. The developer makes charts and graphs informative by loading the data into visualization frameworks, such as Matplotlib or Seaborn. In the process of discovering trends, pattern recognition, and informing stakeholders about what has been discovered, data visualization serves as a very effective technique. In the sense that using a range of formats can easily make it possible for developers to deal with millions and billions of data sets, thus making them represent in ways that are most visually appealing with improved overall effect of their study.

Working with CSV, JSON, and XML data is useful not only for data processing but also for data validation and error management. All operations of processing data must include checks on the correctness and integrity of data from external sources. Such applications, which depend on error-free data like financial systems or medical applications, require special consideration. Developers should include detailed validation tests to avoid any potential errors and corruption of data, with the data satisfying constraints and format anticipated. Error handling is also of great importance when dealing with data formats since several problems may occur when loading and processing the data. Developers are likely to encounter corrupted XML structures, badly formatted JSON data, or faulty CSV files to name but a few examples. These issues can be handled elegantly by having robust error handling procedures in place that report failures and provide end-users with insightful feedback on what caused the failure. These processes do not only make the applications more robust but also improve user experience since they prevent crashes and provide step-by-step instructions on how to troubleshoot the issues.

Newer formats and standards are set to come up because the landscape of data management is still in a flux. The fundamentals of XML, JSON, and CSV data handling will still be there, however. It would always come in handy for developers to be able to read, write, and convert between these formats because it will enable them to move with changes in requirements and changing technology. Indeed, one cannot really talk of the significance of efficient data management techniques without anything to say about how data is becoming increasingly important to businesses, research, and day-to-day decision-making activities. Summarizing, any data analyst and developer necessarily uses CSV, JSON, and XML data. The working of these formats allows continuation of work toward the administration and analysis of data. Each has properties that make it suitable for the range of application. While they are indeed more flexible and extensible to house more complex data structures, there is simply no beating the CSV when it comes to compactly tabular simple data.

Therefore, it is paramount that developers become at home with these core data formats, along with their corresponding tools, as technology is continually advancing. Such less important uses of CSV, JSON, and XML will be scrapped, which will enable organizations to enhance the management and interpretation capabilities with regard to data. The world would see better decisions and innovation as the new king.

CONCLUSION

You have now completed "The Python Programming Revolution: Scripting Success: Practical Approaches to Python Programming," so you've achieved a sound base in the programming world with Python. You have just finished this trip through the basic constructs of Python, from its syntax and control flow to more involved ideas like how to interface with external libraries and object-oriented programming.

Throughout the process, you considered real-world examples, completed useful coding tasks, and gained greater comprehension of the several fields in which Python may be used, such as web development, data analysis, and automation.

This is a versatile language, and at this point, you're ready to do quite a bit of different things within it – from data analysis to development of web applications, automation of tasks, and experimentation with machine learning. When you get into developing and tackling tougher projects, the methods and tools you learned here will be a great advantage.

Remember as you read this book that programming is a constantly evolving field with countless areas to delve into. For further development of your Python abilities, keep exploring new libraries, frameworks, and tools. Built upon the magnificent strategies in this book, you will be a successful scriptwriter well on your way to being a contributor to the growing world of Python programming. Keep on coding, keep on being curious, and have all those chances that Python gives you.

Thank you for buying and reading/ listening to our book. If you found this book useful/ helpful please take a few minutes and leave a review on the platform where you purchased our book. Your feedback matters greatly to us.